PERMISSION EVANGELISM

WHEN TO TALK
WHEN TO WALK

MICHAEL L. SIMPSON

Building the New Generation of Believers

An Imprint of Cook Communications Ministries
Colorado Springs, Colorado

NexGen® is an imprint of
Cook Communications Ministries, Colorado Springs, CO 80918
Cook Communications, Paris, Ontario
Kingsway Communications, Eastbourne, England

PERMISSION EVANGELISM
©2003 by Michael Simpson

First Printing, 2003
Printed in the United States of America
1 2 3 4 5 6 7 8 9 10 Printing/Year 07 06 05 04 03

Editor: Janet L. Lee
Design: Jeffrey P. Barnes

NOTE: Some names have been changed to protect the privacy of the individuals referenced

Library of Congress Cataloging-in-Publication Data

Simpson, Michael (Michael L.), 1965-
   Permission evangelism / Michael Simpson.
      p. cm.
   Includes bibliographical references.
   ISBN 0-7814-3908-6
   1. Evangelistic work. I. Title.
   BV3770.S5 2003
   269'.2--dc21
                                        2003000387

DEDICATION

To my friend and brother in arms, Jeffrey.
You inspired me to follow God's direction and remain
obedient to His calling on my life.

ACKNOWLEDGEMENTS

Thanks for reading this page. I know the majority of the people that peruse this section of a book are friends or family and the people that worked on the project. I wonder can an author thank all those deserving without sounding like the expectant Oscar winner refusing to leave the stage? I guess it doesn't really matter. If you want to know more about me, you need to know of these people.

Connie Clark taught me that approaching conventional wisdom from a different perspective is not only acceptable, but also required. I've learned what it means to be a man of God from some pretty godly men. Peter Grant, Greg Sorenson and Kevin Cash; you were my earliest influences as a new Christian. Your words and grace shown me made an indelible impression. You, along with Dr. William Craig, taught me that my heart and head need not be divorced, but together both can become a force to change the lives of many.

I must say thanks to all those that encouraged, edited and displayed amazing patience as I worked out these words verbally: my fellow ministry partners and friends, Jeffrey, Alisha, Scott, and Jennifer; Noel, for your smiling research; Jon, Dave, and Kevin for your suggestions and thought-provoking insights; and everyone else that prayed me through the process, especially my family. Susan and Tonya, your stories were a blessing to me, and I'm sure will be to others. I greatly appreciate the time and effort all of you invested in this work.

Thanks also to Janet Lee and my new friends at Cook Communications Ministries for acting on their passion for freeing Christians from bondage, sharing God's love with the lost, and for showing faith in me. Your excitement and confidence compelled me.

I pray that all of you are blessed by the words to follow.

CONTENTS

Acknowledgments 5

Introduction 9

1. Why It's Time for Permission 13

2. Understanding the Unbeliever 28

3. Jesus Got It! 43

4. Scared and Feeling Guilty 64

5. Getting Permission 80

6. The Power of Story 101

7. Being in the World 123

8. Grasping God's Heart 137

9. Check Your Motives 151

10. Group Permission—the Role of the Church 165

11. No Silver Bullet 185

Appendix 198

INTRODUCTION

I think I've read them all, and now I've written one—another book on evangelism. You hear about this "duty" in church, Bible studies, bookshelves, and the radio. There are classes, workshops, and conferences, but Christians still dread the word and live a life of guilt. You can't win. Either you feel guilty for interrupting someone and forcing him to listen to your rehearsed questions, or you feel guilty for not wanting to.

Something is terribly wrong with our idea of sharing God's love with the lost if we dread being involved in God's greatest miracle. Evangelism has become a "responsibility," a duty that is avoided on both sides—those giving and receiving. If we believe what the Bible tells us about the salvation of nonbelievers being God's greatest joy, we must be missing the point.

When we live under our own power, everything is work, including evangelism. Evangelism can't be "God's work" unless God is working in the giver of the message and the person on the other end. So, understanding how to discern the Holy Spirit's leading in a nonbeliever should lead to fruitful conversations every time. By redefining success, not in numbers, but in our obedience to God, sometimes walking away is the right thing to do. After all, Jesus never chased anyone down to convince him of his need for salvation.

The big questions are:

How do you know with whom to start a conversation?

How do you relate to today's non-Christian if you have known God most of your life?

How do you communicate the work of grace in your life?

How do you know when to talk and when to walk?

The answer is in *permission*. If someone asks then you can speak *without* fear that you will be rejected. If you get permission, you are then engaged in a give-and-take conversation before you even begin your testimony. Does it sound outrageous that someone would ask you to tell him or her about Jesus? Well, it has happened to me hundreds of times, even in first encounters on short airplane flights. What is equally exciting, though, is that I have been able to walk away from just as many encounters not having talked about my faith without a sense of failure and without alienating that person, because the timing wasn't God's. Time and time again, many of these same people have returned months later and given me permission to continue in our conversation about faith.

We have been taught by Christian culture to interrupt strangers and force people to listen. But that was not the approach Jesus used with the lost. Christ told parables that few understood and let those not seeking truth—or not yet ready to accept truth—walk away. Was he a poor evangelist, or did he know something about relating to the lost that we've somehow missed?

This is not a book for Christians who are not open to new and challenging approaches, and it is not a book for people seeking a silver bullet method for evangelism. This book is about the infectious nature of God's heart and tapping into his plan for using his Spirit in the believer to draw the lost to himself. It's also about rediscovering the joy of our own salvation and wanting to see that joy in others.

Evangelism isn't just important for the non-Christian—it's important for YOU. Sharing the gift of God's love with someone else should be the most exciting and encouraging event in your life—every time it happens. Think of what you may be missing! Be selfish, be greedy, and be relentless with your desire to grow closer to God; but understand that the greatest intimacy with God's heart is found in sharing his greatest passion.

If you desire to know God's heart, you must become enraptured with his greatest passion. When you understand God's heart and let it change you, you can learn to help others discover his grace. If all of heaven rejoices at the salvation of one soul, shouldn't we want to join the party?

Evangelism isn't a duty; it's a blessing. It is an opportunity for you to grow closer to God and know his heart intimately. By learning to discern the working of his Spirit, you will unleash the power of his Spirit in your life. And, it allows you to experience love and grace like nothing else you will ever find in this life.

Do you desire to get the most out of your relationship with God? Then I challenge you to learn how to help fulfill his greatest desire—that none should perish. Do you want to grow in your desire to tell others about the work of Christ in your life today? Then I challenge you to learn how to share your story in a way that engages the heart of others.

My prayer is that within the pages of this book many of you will find renewed joy in loving the non-Christian, that you will be granted freedom to wait for God's timing, and that you will become addicted to sharing the message of grace.

CHAPTER ONE

WHY IT'S TIME FOR PERMISSION

"Hi. Would you be interested in switching over to TMI Long Distance service?"

"Oh, gee, I can't talk right now. Why don't you give me your home number and I'll call you later."

"Uh, sorry, we're not allowed to do that."

"Oh, I guess you don't want people calling you at home."

"No."

"Well, now you know how I feel."

– Telemarketer and Jerry in the Seinfeld *episode "The Pitch"*[1]

Bzzzzzzzzzzzzzzzz ...

I know it's rude, but haven't you ever wanted to deliver the quick retort to the evening telemarketer? If there's one thing that gets under my skin, it is rude interruptions. I have paid extra for an unlisted phone number since I was twenty-five years old for exactly that reason, but they still seem to locate me.

We all hate interruptions, and telemarketers are on the top of our lists of annoyances. Laws are being passed to stop them, and new devices and telephone services to block and identify computer-dialed calls are in high demand. It seems time has a value, and those precious seconds wasted with telemarketing interruptions are worth more than $9.95 a month.

If we hate that kind of interruption so much, consider this one: "Excuse me, can I talk with you for a moment?"

A bit annoyed at the interruption, I reluctantly responded, "Uh, I'm really in a hurry. What about?"

"Do you know for sure that you are going to be with God in heaven?"

"Huh? I know for sure that I'm gonna be late for the game," and my friends and I walked on.

My non-Christian friends scoffed and made general, prejudiced disparaging comments about Christians as we walked away. I was embarrassed, not for my beliefs and being a Christian, but because I was now associated with that experience. My friends knew well what I believed because we often spoke of my faith, but whenever we would run across a street evangelist or hear about Christians in militant activities in the news, they seemed to take a step backward. Eventually, they began to consider me an anomaly in the Christian world, and not necessarily a byproduct of my faith.

I felt bad for walking away from that evangelist outside the stadium because I knew his intentions were honorable and we were brothers in the Lord, but I was even more annoyed at the rude and ill-timed encounter. I'll say it again—I hate interruptions. We get interrupted every day by advertisers, telemarketers, Internet pop-up windows, and countless strangers stealing our precious time, our most valued commodity.

Telemarketers prey on the elderly and uninformed and certainly generate revenue (sometimes through fraud), but I don't know of anyone who has ever bought anything from an errant call. Consequently, although I hear it occasionally happens, I don't think it likely that anyone in a westernized country will accept Christ after being randomly stopped on a busy street for a night on the town. I do, however, personally know of hundreds of people that have been loved into salvation.

Not for Naught—But Not Enough

Sometimes God resurrects those random remarks later in life, so I'll never say they aren't worthwhile, but they rarely bear fruit short-term. And I wonder if they are the best use of your time in your relationships with non-Christians. The world yells at us in the activity of life, yet God whispers in the quiet moments. God touches our hearts most often in solitude and quiet conversation, the confusing calm after major interruptions of death, illness, or loss, and the paralyzing fear of life's foxholes. You meet God when you are still and questioning, and he is faithful to bring the answers when you actively look for truth. Elijah discovered God's presence manifested in the soft whisper of his voice, not in the outward displays of his power (1 Kings 19:11-13). In learning to listen for his Spirit, we lose our requirement for signs.

Christ claimed that he was "the way and the truth and the life" (John 14:6). *To want a way, you have to have selected a desired destination. Anyone who is looking for truth has asked a question. All people who found life in Christ once considered their life wanting.* These are all volitional acts of the will, mind, and heart. That's why Christ never chased anyone down to hear the promise of salvation. He knew when to talk and when to walk and instructed his disciples to shake the dust off their sandals and walk on when they came upon a town resistant to the message of God (Luke 10:10-11).

The disciples experienced resistance, but it was not from the people whose hearts were willing to hear; it was from the people who were threatened by their success in reaching the lost. They endured hardship for the sake of those seeking truth and never forced their message on those resistant. If God whispers, Christ reveals himself to those who actively seek truth, and the disciples were instructed to speak with gentle yet respectful confidence, why then do we expect people to respond positively to interruptions and arguments?

Evangelism as most people know it is an unnatural act. Christians knock on strangers' doors, interrupting their time with their family, stop random people in the street, divert vacationers' enjoyment, and flash Bible verses at sporting events. Others stand on street corners spouting the promise of eternal damnation at passersby with a white-knuckled grip on a well-worn Bible, which appears more as a weapon than a beacon of hope.

Good intentions, even with poor delivery, will occasionally bear results if there's persistence. Just like in the corporate world, even bad marketing will gain you a customer once in a while. We should celebrate those victories of God, but that does not mean we shouldn't make the most of our time and never settle for the occasional happening. We should be compelled to do evangelism with excellence.

~~Living~~ Thriving with the Label

Failure and rejection are demoralizing, but we are told that sharing our faith is our duty. As faithful, grace-filled Christians, we battle in conversation and relationship against the scars and social impressions left by the extremes of the ambivalent and unchanged so-called Christians, as well as those blaspheming the name of God through violence, hate, and greed.

Because of our "Christian" label, our promise of hope and grace, more often than not, falls on deaf ears. Ours is a society resistant to listening and increasingly unwilling to walk through the doors of our churches to seek answers to life and death. The joy of sharing the promise of life with God has been sucked out of the Christian culture, and many of us cringe at the idea of evangelism. And all our wishing that it wasn't so doesn't change a thing. We long for an imagined day of true religious freedom and eager hearts in our own country.

In our postmodern, post-Christian society, with its "coincidental" breakdown of the family structure, multiple generations have missed out on the wonder of the power and love of God. We are not a story-telling society anymore, but rather an information-receiving people. Today's view of the impact of Christ on the Christian is molded not by family stories but by headlines and news stories about those who claim to know God, yet threaten and shame God's name because of their sin. "For years, Christians have enjoyed a 'favored nation' status within our culture. This is largely because, due to our numbers and influence, we have virtually created a cultural soil on which we stand. That soil is changing. Christians are just beginning to wake up to the growing impatience, animosity, and even open hostility our culture now shows to Christians."[2]

Time for a Change

The cultural gap that generates a twisted view of God and waters down the impact of Christ on a person's life demands we carry the stories of God and the promise of hope outside the confines of the organized church. We need to be ready for when we encounter people who seek spirituality but reject organized religion.

Today, most nonbelievers were not brought up in the culture of the church and do not seek answers there. They don't share a common set of beliefs—they don't speak the language. The church wants to give them answers to questions they aren't even asking. Without a new approach, evangelism will continue to be a burden, and churches will remain largely unsuccessful in their efforts to reach the non-Christian. Therefore, the organized church itself cannot successfully be the bearer of the promise of salvation on a grand scale as it once thought.

In the past, church was part of our national identity as a Christian country, and people saw the church as a place to have spiritual needs met and where rules for moral conduct were established. Most nonbelievers shared in a common belief base—yes, there is a God; yes, the Bible is true; and, of course I want to go to heaven when I die. The church was viewed as the "answer place" and the church was the primary instrument of evangelism.

For massive change to occur, the church must shift its focus from igniting revival in the millions of people dead to hope in Christ, to empowering every Christian to be a monument to God's grace on the paths the common man travels. This culture's seeker must see the results of the power of God in the life of an individual and ask to know the story of a Christian equipped and willing to share.

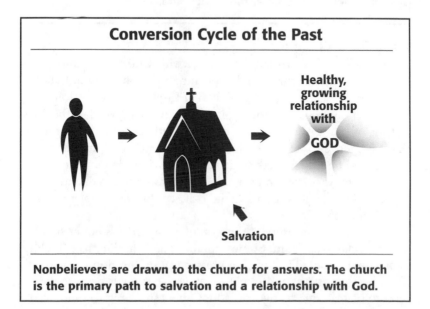

Conversion Cycle of the Past

Healthy, growing relationship with

GOD

Salvation

Nonbelievers are drawn to the church for answers. The church is the primary path to salvation and a relationship with God.

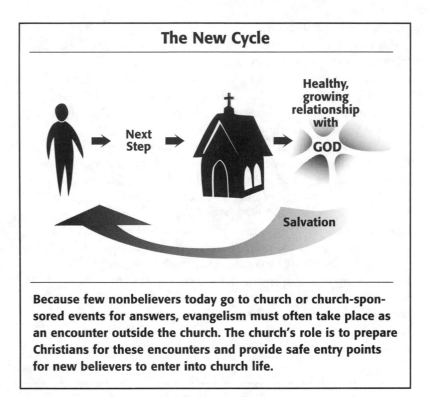

The New Cycle

Next Step → 🏠 → Healthy, growing relationship with GOD

Salvation

Because few nonbelievers today go to church or church-sponsored events for answers, evangelism must often take place as an encounter outside the church. The church's role is to prepare Christians for these encounters and provide safe entry points for new believers to enter into church life.

Need for a Change

After becoming a Christian, I saw a life with Christ as the most amazing experience that could happen to a person. Why didn't everyone else see it so clearly? Why had I rejected it for so long? My church, although I thought it was great, had growth difficulties outside of luring Christians from other churches, and I soon found that experience to be commonplace. After inviting my friends to church and finding few takers, it became obvious to me that there was something awry with how the church was perceived, and I wondered if evangelism on a grand scale could ever happen within those confines.

How do you measure the success of a church? It's not as simple as the weekly seat count. Some churches play a healing role, cycling people in and out. They serve a great purpose, but don't reach many non-Christians and rarely show sizable growth because they tend to plateau due to the rotation. Others show regular and even extreme growth but are only luring disgruntled or bored Christians from other churches with elaborate productions and programs. Still others are growing the old-fashioned way—people changed by grace, inviting others into the process.

How is the growth in your church? Are real, unchurched, non-Christians attending, or are your outreach efforts just pulling in the marginal Christian? Why do people go to church, anyway? Why do they not? How does your faith experience resemble the rest of America? Knowing how your experience compares is not just a job for your pastors and leaders; it is critical to understanding the unchurched and the roadblocks you may encounter in connecting with them outside of church.

There was a momentary increase in church attendance across the United States in the late 1980s when the Baby Boomers with childhood church history returned once married and began reproducing. After that, church attendance dropped almost 20 percent between 1991 and 2000.[3] If you think that's disturbing, check out these numbers:

- Median church size adult attendance (100 people) dropped 10 percent from 1997 to 1999.[4]
- People in their thirties are now 35 percent less likely to attend church as the generation in their forties.[5]
- Out of those claiming to be Christian, teens are half as likely as adults to claim to be "absolutely committed to the Christian faith."[6]
- 62 percent of people that have not attended church in over six months claim to be Christian[7]
- "seven out of ten adults have no clue what "John 3:16" means."[8]
- Probability of accepting Christ between the ages of:
    > 5 and 13 is 32 percent.
    > 14 and 18 is 4 percent
    > and over 18 years of age is just 6 percent [9]

The situation appears bleak. Church attendance is trending down, but these statistics are merely early indicators that may worsen through time. Single people are 37 percent less likely to attend church than those married[10], and the desire to stay single or marry later in life is increasing. In addition, since overwhelmingly more Christian conversions happen as children, and adults who attended church regularly as a child are three times more likely to attend as adults, the decline in childhood church attendance will incur heavy casualties ten to twenty years from now.

As children become adults and begin seeking spiritual truth, it is increasingly unlikely they will consider the Christian church as a viable option. All indicators show that barring radical transformation in the perceptions of the populous regarding Christianity, the Christian church in westernized countries is in for a long, cold winter. How did it get this bad, and who's responsible?

Why the Change?

I believe that Christ being less attractive than the world is a byproduct of a diluted view of Christianity. People who claim to be Christian but have never committed their life to Christ and received the Holy Spirit, make up a significant portion of the "so-called" Christian community. This has led to a view that Christians are minimally, if at all, positively changed by God. The resulting impact, when grace in the Christian is not evident, is to not seek change and grace through Christ.

There are certainly people that refuse love and will not respond to honest compassion and caring at some point in their lives, but the bulk of humanity craves purpose and love right now. They just don't believe it is available within the Christian church, and no wonder. When has a zealous "so-called" Christian ever accepted them, respected them, or loved them?

Most adult nonbelievers, I am sad to say, will not toil long in completing that list. But when asked about their experiences of judgment, hate, simple alienation, criticism, and shame at the hands of people claiming to be Christians, you better clear your calendar. I doubt any of you are responsible for these negative perceptions because you obviously have a heart to reach the lost or you wouldn't be reading this book, but these perceptions are reality and we must consider them. Do not be alarmed, I am not stepping upon the soapbox of justice to reprimand the church for these atrocities, but I will shine the light on them because they are the canvas with which those of us who desire to reach the lost must paint.

After the horrific destruction of the World Trade Center in New York City on September 11, 2001, the media has been keenly interested in the role of religion in helping American's cope with these confusing, saddening times. One such research project garnered the cover of *U.S. News and World Report* in May of 2002. The results may surprise you.

According to this poll, 84.2 percent of Americans claim to be Christians. That's 159 million people! "That's great," you say; "We should focus our evangelism outside the United States." Unfortunately, it is not that clear cut. *U.S. News and World Report* revealed the sobering truth in its 2002 poll where it stated that only 19 percent of people claiming to be Christians believe the religion they practice is the only *true* religion.[11] If you are aware of the claims of Christ, "I am the way and the truth and the life. No one comes to the Father except through me" (John 14:6), and believe the Bible to be true, then you should find that disturbing. It would be less troubling if the people who are claiming to be Christian also claim to believe what you believe. The problem is that most do not.

The majority of people who claim to be Christian don't accept the biblical definition of Christianity. Therefore, you can't expect that they are Christians. "Duh," you say. "There's no revelation in that statement." Well, there may not be, but when we look at the ramifications of this cultural sea change and how it impacts the future of evangelism and Christianity in America, it becomes much more interesting.

Many a famous quote exists concerning statistics, most unfit to print. Wilhelm Stekel said, "Statistics is the art of lying by the means of numbers." Even so, as a marketing executive, I saw data and statistics as oxygen—no data, no survival. Incorrect data that is consistently incorrect proves valuable; the key is to know what is wrong and to follow the changes and patterns, not the absolutes. The statistics I quoted earlier are very misleading, but reveal the heart of the problem concerning Christian evangelism in westernized countries, especially America.

To understand how to interpret those statistics so we can get a more accurate view of Christianity and non-Christians, we must understand what qualifies as modern *statistical Christianity:*

Groups which self-identify as part of Christianity include (but are not limited to): African Independent Churches (AICs), the Aglipayan Church, Amish, Anglicans, Armenian Apostolic, Assemblies of God; Baptists, Calvary Chapel, Catholics, Christadelphians, Christian Science, the Community of Christ, the Church of Jesus Christ of Latter-day Saints, Coptic Christians, Eastern Orthodox churches, Ethiopian Orthodox, Evangelicals, Iglesia ni Cristo, Jehovah's Witnesses, the Local Church, Lutherans, Methodists, Nestorians, the New Apostolic Church, Pentecostals, Plymouth Brethren, Presbyterians, the Salvation Army, Seventh-Day Adventists, Shakers, Stone-Campbell churches (Disciples of Christ, Churches of Christ, the "Christian Church and Churches of Christ," the International Church of Christ), Uniate churches, United Church of Christ/Congregationalists, the Unity Church, Universal Church of the Kingdom of God, Vineyard churches, and others. These groups exhibit varying degrees of similarity, cooperation, and communion with other groups. None are known to consider all other Christian sub-groups to be equally valid. David Barrett, an Evangelical Christian who is the compiler of religion statistics for the *Encyclopedia Britannica,* includes all of the groups listed above in the worldwide statistics for Christianity (source: www.adherents.com).[12]

The basics of Christianity (Jesus Christ is the Son of God; the New Testament account of his life as true; salvation is by grace alone and not works of any kind, etc.) are the foundation of the church and transcend all truly Christian denominations regardless of their personal traditions and political views. Although a clear dividing line for believers, these delineations are mere subtleties to mainstream culture and written off as infighting and petty arguments. Considering that just about any religion that claims some acceptance of the New Testament and Jesus Christ as a miracle-worker is considered part of the greater Christian church, thus being included in modern statistical research, we must draw the conclusion that these statistics are woefully skewed.

Unfortunately, in this case, it likely makes for increasingly negative results. That 19 percent of "Christians" claiming their religion is the only "true" religion is certainly made up of many groups most Christians would not include as peers in belief. Dare I say that Mormons and Jehovah's Witnesses are more prone, as a collective, to make this statement than most of the Evangelical Christian church? Together, they number in the millions, and along with other sects and the ever-present ambivalent, Sunday-only Christian, will forever skew the viewpoint of Christianity in America, thus impacting your ability to accurately represent Christ.

I have taught at numerous churches that have fantastic international missions programs that show great results abroad but little evangelism training or enthusiasm to reach their own neighbors and friends. American churches' outreach programs have traditionally been focused on reaching the lost outside our country's borders and healing the Christians within. But that type of evangelism strategy leaves out the bulk of our society today.

Of course, progress in other countries is easier to see even when success has come as the result of plans and commitments years in the making. This is true mainly because the stark contrast of a face that has passed from dark to light is so profoundly different. I remember standing in a Russian train terminal with hundreds of people waiting for two friends of a missionary I was visiting, wondering how I would recognize them. They were Russian, but Christian, and when they arrived in the terminal I easily pointed them out. Their clothes were the same as the myriad strangers about them, but their faces were different. They glowed in comparison. It was a sight I will never forget.

Being light in darkness is considerably easier to understand when everyone else isn't impersonating light. It is different in our world where the needs of people are generally met, and everyone pretends to be happy and "together." It is difficult to identify the "true" Christian in the workplace or neighborhood, so most people rely on the Christian caricatures presented by the media. To have an impact, or even an introduction, we must be the antithesis of the media representation. Making others question their point of view about Christians is often a necessary step to questioning whether truth can be found in Christ.

Christ voraciously attacked the Pharisees in public primarily because he wanted his followers to understand he was not challenging them to become like their hypocritical leaders. He was promising they could become something better. What would Christ say today about the purity of our worship and motives? It's worth thinking about.]

What Is Evangelism?

Evangelism has no synonyms, and is by popular definition *militant zeal*. The word and its definition are modern man's creation, not God's, and I believe we have missed the point. God intended our zeal for reaching others to be born of our personal experience with him, filling us with such great peace of the Holy Spirit that we must often respond to questions concerning our evident hope. The evidence of the Holy Spirit in our lives is the proof of our relationship with God. (John 15:26-27; 16:13-16). Biblical evangelism is certainly zeal, but it is born of joy, peace, and God's heart for the lost, not aggression acted out by a misguided sense of duty. To me, evangelism is as much *selfish*, for lack of a better word, as it is responsible.

If you define all healthy relationships as "an ever-increasing knowledge of each other," which includes equal growth in knowledge of yourself, then relationships stagnate and die when one or both of you feel there is nothing else to know, or lose the desire to discover more. God's great design for our ever-growing knowledge of him is dependent upon experiencing his love in the process of someone else's salvation. I'm convinced that our relationship with God can be fulfilling, but never complete, without loving others in this way (Matt. 22:37-40, Phil. 2:1-5).

When God said he gives us the desires of our hearts (Ps. 37:4), he didn't mean that he gives us whatever we ask for. He meant that *his* desires are placed in our hearts by *him*, and then fulfilled. God desires lost people to be in relationship with him, and he desires us to love our neighbors as ourselves. If loving yourself and loving God means growing in knowledge of God, you are called to love your neighbor in the same way. When our relationship is such that our desires align with God's, we must attain his heart for reaching the lost. If we do not have this desire, we are short-changing our experience with God.

All of these points define evangelism as responses to the movement of the Spirit, not coercive actions by man. In their writings, John Edwards, John Piper, and Sam Storms have referred to the unequaled joy found in passionate service to God as "Christian Hedonism," and I wouldn't attempt to rebrand it. This same perspective on looking at fulfilling our perceived duty to God differently applies to evangelism. The enjoyment of God found through the involvement in someone else's salvation process is as unequaled in joy as the most intense worship or healing you will ever experience.

Doing Our Duty

Most Christians today labor under the burden of what is commonly known as the "Great Commission" in Matthew 28:

"Therefore go and make disciples of all nations, baptizing them in the name of the Father and of the Son and of the Holy Spirit, and teaching them to obey everything I have commanded you" (vv. 19-20a).

Given that charge, I agree that Christians have a "duty" to evangelize, and it appears rather weighty. And it sounds like it is 100 percent up to us to get the job done. Christ left, and now it's our responsibility, right?

Wrong!

Why do we so often stop there? What's missing? If we investigate Christ's entire thought, we get a more accurate and telling direction:

"Then Jesus came to them and said, 'All authority in heaven and on earth has been given to me. Therefore go and make disciples of all nations, baptizing them in the name of the Father and of the Son and of the Holy Spirit, and teaching them to obey everything I have commanded you. And surely I am with you always, to the very end of the age'" (vv. 18-20).

The missing pieces are the bookends to our assigned task—Christ has all authority in heaven and on earth, and Christ hasn't left—he is with us always. Yes, he is sending his disciples (us) out into the world to reach unbelievers and be involved in their salvation process. But he also lets us know that he has the authority, we are working on his behalf, and he is always with us. How can he be with us always?

The Bible says we are one with Christ; we have died and have been resurrected with Christ (Rom. 6:4-5); we are equal heirs with Christ (Rom. 8:16-17); and Christ left his Spirit to be with us

25

always. The difference is that we are still physically here, and he isn't, right? Not exactly. If we are one with Christ, we are one with Christ, period. As believers, we are the physical manifestation of Christ's heart and efforts to reach the lost on earth we provide much more than you may think.

"No one can come to me unless the Father who sent me draws him" (John 6:44).

First, God woos the lost and calls them to Christ, not bodily, but *Holy Spiritually*. Second, Christ is with us always, manifested as the Spirit in the believer. Therefore, it is reasonable to conclude that God's Spirit draws them to US! Unbelievers are not led to us for their ultimate salvation because we cannot provide that, but we are expected and designed to be part of the process.

Our Real Calling

We are called to "Always be prepared to give an answer to everyone who asks you to give the reason for the hope that you have. But do this with gentleness and respect, keeping a clear conscience" (1 Peter 3:15b-16a).

We are called by God to be responsive, gentle, and respectful, but are taught by our churches to interrupt strangers, argue, debate, and defend our beliefs. Consequently, we find little joy in sharing our hope, and we communicate even less. Because of these methods, our fear of driving our friends and family away causes us to quietly retreat or aggressively attack and hope for the best. Whether it is our fear, our guilt for not doing our duty, or a true lack of compassion for the lost, every day that we do not share in God's greatest passion is a day we have missed an opportunity to know him more intimately.

This day, and for the rest of your life, seek to know God better and identify his touch on everything and every person you encounter. You love yourself by loving God and by helping those you encounter know the same joy. God has chosen to use me in the lives of many people, but it was not always that way. When I first became a Christian, it took me quite a while to figure out why my efforts at evangelism bore so little fruit. Fortunately, God opened my eyes to a better way and nothing in my life, or in the lives of those I have met since, has ever been the same.

1. Telemarketer and Jerry in the Seinfeld episode, "The Pitch,"
   Written by: Larry David
   Directed by: Tom Cherones
   Broadcasted: September 16, 1992 for the first time.
   Sony Pictures Entertainment

2. Tim Downs in "Finding Common Ground," p. 25, ©1999, Moody Press.

3. Barna Research, "Church Attendance" research archive: "Attendance rose steadily, reaching a peak of 49% in 1991, before beginning a very slow but steady descent back to 40% in January, 2000."

4. ibid, "The 1999 median of 90 adult attenders is down 10% from the 1997 average of 100 attenders, and down 12% from 1992 (102 adult attenders)."

5. ibid, "Baby Busters are least likely to attend church in a typical weekend (only 28%) versus Baby Boomers (43%), Builders (50%) and Seniors (52%). (2000)."

6. Barna Research, Press Release, January 10, 2000, "Teenagers Embrace Religion but Are Not Excited About Christianity", "Three key measures of faith further reveal the true nature of the spirituality of teens. Although four out of five say they are Christian, only one out of four (26%) also claims to be "absolutely committed to the Christian faith." That is only about half the percentage found among adults—and a strong indicator of the flagging depth of loyalty Americans have in relation to its dominant faith group."

7. Barna Research, "One Out of Three Adults is Now Unchurched," February 25, 1999.

8. Barna Research Online, "Evangelism," http://www.barna.org/cgi-bin/ PageCategory. asp#TOP.

9. ibid, Probability of accepting Christ, segmented by age:

   • Children between the ages of 5 and 13 have a 32% probability of accepting Jesus Christ as their savior.

   • The probability of accepting Christ drops to 4% for those who are between the ages of 14 and 18.

   • Those older than 18 have a 6% probability of accepting Jesus Christ as their savior.

10. Barna Research Press Release March 11, 2002, "A Revealing Look at Three Unique Single Adult Populations"

   "In other words, only one-third of single adults (35%) have become "born again" - that is, they no longer trust in their own good deeds as a means to reconciliation with God, but rely completely upon God's grace for their eternal destiny. Never-been-married adults are the least likely to meet the "born again" criteria. In fact, single adults from all three segments are less likely to be born again than are married people."

11. U.S. News and World Report, May 6, 2002, "Faith in America" pgs. 42-43; Religion and Ethics Newsweekly/U.S. News and World Report poll of 2002 adults conducted by Milofsky International and Edison Media Research, March 26-April 4, 2002.

12. Groups which self-identify as part of Christianity include ...   Copyright www.adherents.com
   http://www.adherents.com/Religions_By_Adherents.html#Christianity.

CHAPTER TWO

UNDERSTANDING THE UNBELIEVER

"The history of art is simply a history of getting rid of the ugly by entering into it and using it. After all, the notion of something outside of us being ugly is not outside of us, but inside of us. We are working with our minds trying to get them open so that we don't see things as being ugly, or beautiful, but we see them just as they are."[1]

–John Cage

Matthew 7:1-2

"Do not judge, or you too will be judged. For in the same way you judge others, you will be judged, and with the measure you use, it will be measured to you."

Three hours of flying and we were farther from our destination than when we began. The conversation with Jim had started innocently enough. But some time after the small talk concerning our business trip led to an open discussion about our religious beliefs, it all went wrong. He seemed shocked that I was aware of the closely held and supposedly secretive rituals of his LDS faith. He was ashamed that I knew more of his religion's historical basis than he did. My arguments were convincing and true, but he became increasingly angry and irrational as the flight continued. After awhile he turned away and stared out the window, refusing to

28

engage, indicating his distaste for my words. As a Christian desiring to fulfill my call to share God's love and truly desiring Jim to know the joy I'd found in Christ, his reaction crushed me. I had been preparing for that conversation for over a year prior, since I first heard my employer might relocate me to Utah. But when I left the plane that day, I was confused and I felt like a failure.

Jim and I continued to work together for years, but we never spoke of God or religion again. What went wrong? Did I just not understand Mormons, or had I become so alienated from non-Christians since accepting Christ that nobody but a Christian could relate to me?It was the first conversation about our beliefs that my colleague and I had ever engaged in. We'd known each other for a while and shared a mutual respect. We had just completed a very successful business trip that created one of those bonds of camaraderie resulting from the shared experience of surviving a battle and coming out the victors. We were laughing and enjoying each other's company when the words he chose revealed he desired to get to know me on a more personal level. The time was right to bridge the conversation to God. At least, that's what the plethora of evangelism training courses and books had taught me.

I did everything *right*, at least as far as I had been taught. I knew my subject and knew my Bible. The conversation easily led toward spiritual things, and I spoke with supposed wisdom. I didn't attack and tried to avoid argument but logically kept to the issues. I never became defensive, remained confident, and even expressed genuine empathy. Still, something was wrong, and it wasn't just with his belief system.

After returning home, I couldn't rest and was plagued with that conversation for days. My angst forced a choice: I could try again, although he was unlikely to let me; write him off as too obstinate and pray that someone else would reach him; or ask God to give me wisdom and enlightenment. I prayed something like this, "Lord, there are so many people who don't know you: Mormons, Muslims, Buddhists, Satanists, atheists, agnostics, and the like. How can I know what to say to them all? Am I to just reach one people group in my life and ignore the rest of humanity? Lord, give me discernment and wisdom. *Help me to understand your Spirit and what each person I meet needs to hear.* Amen."

Within days my quest began in earnest, rooted in unexpected circumstances. At the time I was developing and teaching a class for my church, combining the best of my past instruction on evangelism and apologetics. I had recently sensed that the course was missing something—something that until now I hadn't even realized should be included. With only one exception, the class was comprised of ten Christians that had all accepted Christ as children. I had intended to teach *adult* converts how to reach their friends and family since that was my story. I was unaware of the depth of insecurity and fear that people who had grown up in the church had about sharing their faith.

As we discussed their fears about evangelism, one point became quite evident. These life-long believers didn't understand the adult non-Christian—what they were thinking. We began to engage in a very prayerful, yet analytical look at people who don't know God. Just as I had learned when attempting to reach a new "market" in business, we sought common denominators to guide our prayers and words. What we decided is that most people fall into one of two camps.

Two Camps

I loathe when someone places me in a box as much as the next person, but as my years in business have taught me, effectively reaching your target audience means understanding their common characteristics so you can specifically address them. So at the risk of being labeled as one of those people that oversimplifies, I have to say that from the perspective of religious belief, all people, including Christians, can be included in one of two camps:

1. *Can* concisely articulate what they believe (Firm Group) or
2. *Can't* concisely articulate what they believe (Flexible Group)

This is valuable to know because your approach to addressing them will vary depending on where they stand. Every individual—from nonbeliever to committed Christian—will fall into one of these two groups. Of course, what someone claims to be, and the biblical definition of his or her spiritual state, may greatly differ.

30

Regardless of their salvation situation, if the people God puts in your path are not in a healthy, growing relationship with God, the objective is to guide them there. The objective and the methods are exactly the same—biblically and relationally. For the Christian and the non-Christian alike, it's all about admitting your need, asking forgiveness, turning from sin, and trusting God. But because this book is about helping you to make the kind of connection with people that puts you in a position to guide and challenge them, you will need to adjust your methods for individuals in each group.

The Firm Group

In the first group, which we'll call the "firm" group, are individuals who are likely to be involved in some organized religion, or have been at one time in their lives. This group is statistically smaller than the "flexible" group described next. Individuals in this group tend to be firmly involved in community and are most comfortable with a faith that is steeped in education and relatively strict. Because of their involvement in a close community, they may fear emotional, social, financial, and in some cases, physical ramifications for rejecting their faith or not fully participating as expected. Though rarely acknowledged verbally, those social truths are well understood within their cultures. Don't think this just happens in third world countries. It is more common in mainstream western religions than you might think.

These people are often more willing to engage in a discussion about spiritual matters because they have some level of confidence in their religious knowledge and may even have a desire to convert you. Because they have numerous statements of belief as points of discussion (e.g., Islam claims that Christ was merely a prophet, like Mohammed, and not God), traditional apologetic arguments may seem the natural way to go. However, these types of arguments are less likely to result in a positive or continuing discussion, unless adversarial. Try to employ the techniques introduced later in the book concerning redirecting debate in order to move the conversation to a more productive place.

While conversations are often easier to start with someone from the "firm" group, making progress is usually much more frustrating and difficult. Of course, that is never a reason to avoid those conversations. Just make sure you're patient and prayerful. Unlearning a lifetime of teaching is much more difficult than starting from scratch.

The Flexible Group

The second camp, or the "flexible" group, may or may not have had a religious background. Some consider themselves followers of a particular faith and are quite knowledgeable about its tenets, but don't actively practice its beliefs. Although they may argue this point, being flexible, they pick and choose their beliefs. Their belief choices are usually based on convenience or founded on lifestyle choices.

Others in the flexible camp might not have as much religious history. They have selected what they want—what they deem comfortable for their lives at the time—from a variety of "spiritual" sources or religious experiences. There is so much to choose from, many just select a little of everything appealing and avoid all the foul-looking organizations and rules. Then they stir it all up into their own personal religious dish, a kind of God stew. A great deal of these people claim to be Christian. But with so many claiming to be Christian today who are in reality not (see chapter 1), you may need to ask questions to find out what someone means when he says he is a Christian. The impact of the fluid definition of Christianity impacts every conversation you have about God with a nonbeliever.

What Are You?

Like it or not, the word "Christian" has been poisoned in America. It is not a word that we should abandon, but that word will never save anyone. That word will never draw you closer to anyone but another Christian. When you have earned the respect of another person, claim what you will, but until then be wary of Christian argot that closes relational doors. Sensitivity does not presuppose that you compromise your faith.

When someone initially asks me what I believe, I rarely declare that I am a Christian until I know a little about that person's belief system. Shocked? Let me explain why. Until I know the person's preconceived notion of Christianity, I risk branding myself with his or her potentially incorrect perception and abruptly ending the conversation. I have replied, "I believe in Jesus Christ," "I have a personal relationship with God," and even, "I'm a reformed antagonist," just to get a conversation started. All too often, a response of "I'm a Christian" has put an end to a conversation with someone who was certainly interested in spiritual things.

Don't get me wrong. I will never hide my faith, but it is crucial to speak in a way that invites conversation rather than repels it. If anyone asks if I am a Christian, I will certainly tell him, but I might first ask him, "How do you define a Christian?" Interestingly, this seems to annoy only the Christians I meet. But with non-Christians, it has led directly to telling them about my relationship with Christ and how I came to change my perspective on God, church, and Christianity. By first engaging in understanding their concept of Christianity, I create just enough interest to pull them into conversation. When I finally do state that I am a Christian, based on a clear understanding of what that means to both of us, nonbelievers are often more willing to listen because I have been thoughtful enough to consider their perspective.

Think of it this way. At a coffee shop one day, you meet a modestly dressed elderly man, and you spend the afternoon talking with him. He takes great interest in you. He seems so unselfish, so unencumbered by material cares that you are deeply moved by his humility and kindness. Intrigued, you begin to question his background—how he came to acquire such a kind heart and great wisdom. As soon as he speaks his name, you recognize it from months of media coverage. He is a famous millionaire businessman whose purported greed has left a wake of broken people and controversial business dealings. You are shocked—the name doesn't seem to fit the man with whom you have been interacting.

Later, when telling your friends about this encounter, what will you most recall? If you are like most people, how his true self forced you to change the perception created by the media will consume your thoughts. You will shake your head, tell them how this man was nothing like you had imagined, and how if you had known who he was before you spent time with him, you likely never would have made the effort. You would have missed out on a terrific afternoon because of somebody else's perception.

Successful conversation with non-Christians is best performed with an understanding of their perceptions of the "brand" Christians. Dispelling the incorrect, prejudiced, and negative perceptions, at least as pertain to you, takes the focus off of the negative barriers to listening to truth. Knowing where someone stands—what his own beliefs are, accurate or not—is where you want to head because his path to salvation begins with *his* life experience. What you want to do is let your conversation follow the route of his experiences. This is his spiritual journey, not yours.

Where Have All the Atheists Gone?

As a former atheist, I respect committed atheists and love discussing science and evidence for the existence of God with them. I never fail to be amazed at how much faith they have in scientific theory and how unwilling they are to apply the same principles of drawing logical conclusions when seeking spiritual answers. What I have always appreciated is that a good atheist usually has well thought out arguments. Atheists' issues are basic scientific or logical points, usually a short list, surrounded with big philosophical thoughts supported by somebody else's data. Unfortunately, it is becoming increasingly difficult to get even atheists to articulate the details of their beliefs without significant effort.

Being a byproduct of the dying Modernist society, atheists appear to be reaching extinction outside of the philosophical and scientific elite. In a Barna Research study, only 7 percent of the adult population of the United States (about 14 million people), describe themselves as atheists or agnostics.[2]

"The study also discovered that many of these individuals describe themselves incorrectly. Many atheists are actually agnostics—they believe in some type of deity but are indifferent about the existence of a divine being. (A significant share of those people believes that humans actually possess the power or qualities of gods.) Likewise, many self-proclaimed agnostics are actually atheists—individuals who contend that there is no deity of any type."[3]

Are people today lazy or just confused? How disappointing that we can't even count on the atheists to provide a firm foundation from which to base our arguments. Just like the bulk of society, they have elected to make their own way, because either they just haven't come across a path that looks appealing, or they believe there is no absolute truth (other than Christianity being absolutely false, of course). After all, when there is no absolute truth, the journey is the destination.

Our fickle, noncommittal society seems to require the freedom to change your mind on a whim. Just check out the rising age of first marriages and repetitive divorce statistics if you question the validity of that statement. Where you are today is usually more comfortable to grasp and understand than where you are going. Lack of commitment also gives you the flexibility to change course for whatever reason and as often as you so choose.

My Apology for Arguing

I've found that with the flexible group, apologetics[4] arguments just don't deliver results very well. Actually, they would if you could ever get anyone to engage, but it just doesn't work that way very often. I often sat in a class with a brilliant and well-published Christian philosopher and learned a great deal about constructing arguments. He would present a common statement of what a non-Christian might believe and artfully yank the philosophic rug, as we pictured our imaginary antagonist falling to the ground. A statement like "there is no absolute truth" is a great example. If somebody says that, you can merely ask, "Do you believe that absolutely?" Regardless of the answer, the person either refutes his or her own statement, or deems it useless. A fool is quickly branded.

Although I see apologetics arguments as very valuable with someone truly seeking to remove long-standing barriers to belief, I have found them often distasteful in the early stages of conversation. The problem I've encountered is that most people will rarely make an emphatic, concise statement constructed well enough to dissect. Therefore, you must coerce them into claiming something they don't want to say by summarizing on their behalf. If you haven't earned the right to speak in this manner, or if they have a dislike for philosophical argument (as many do), they usually recognize this as manipulative, then disengage or become defensive. We'll discuss how to avoid that later on, but for now, the important thing to know is that the overwhelming majority of today's society can't concisely articulate what they believe or why they believe it. So what is there to argue about?

Counter Choices

I was a member of the flexible camp before I accepted Christ and after I began to broaden my point of view beyond atheism. After hours of grilling a Christian friend and debating every point I could about her faith, she turned the tables. She simply said, "We've been discussing what I believe and why I believe it all night. Now it's your turn. Tell me what history and science you base your beliefs on." I began well, but after a few minutes it all unraveled, without her uttering a word. I was mortified. I fancied myself an atheist, but the reality was I merely lived and argued as a confused antagonist. I had a childhood background as a traditional Southern Baptist and later in life learned of eastern religions, Christian Science, and traditional rituals from Episcopalian, Presbyterian, and Catholic beliefs. I had concocted a nice God stew but had no solid basis for that perspective.

I certainly didn't believe in Christ or the Bible, but I had left the door open—there could be a God—even though I often claimed no belief apart from science and Darwinian Theory. I mixed up my own concoction and through time had acquired a taste for it, but when called on to share with another, it suddenly didn't sit well. Yet I expected my friend to perfectly defend every aspect of her faith simply because she had chosen. I was a hypocrite, and I was embarrassed. If it hadn't been for my deep-seeded desire to "win," I probably would have walked away in shame and never pursued truth, as so many do when confronted with their sin.

Like myself in those days, many people make decisions on what to believe not because of the merits of the actual belief, but because it contradicts a belief that is distasteful. They choose to NOT believe in the Bible and Christ, or organized religion, because of negative perceptions of the people that take that path. Those paths, in their minds, clearly lead to judgmental and exclusionary attitudes and are associated with close-minded, uneducated, hypocritical people. That not being the chosen destination of most self-respecting people, they feel they have few solid options.

Ask the person driving the vehicle with the ever-popular Darwin fish adorning the bumper whether they consider micro or macro evolution more accurate, and wait for the blank stare. Odds are that person doesn't have a clue what Darwinian theory is beyond "man came from monkeys." In fact, he probably even believes there is a higher power or God. What he probably does believe is that Christians are stupid so he chose the most obvious symbol to counter Christian expression.

For many nonbelievers, their "statement" isn't so much about what they are *for* but a statement *against* what they believe about Christians. Most don't even know exactly what they believe, but are resistant to Christianity because they have bought into the stories of extreme, unloving acts by people that claim to be Christians. They lash out at all Christians indiscriminately using the one thing that seems clearly counter to their views. It rarely occurs to them that kind and decent people they might actually respect and enjoy would be offended.

Like the bulk of the western world, and particularly people in America, they choose what feels good, toss aside what doesn't, and ridicule what they disagree with. They play games with spiritual truth, seeking to manufacture comfort instead of honestly discovering reality, resulting in a religious platypus of sorts; being cute and cuddly, but not really fitting together very well.

How Does All This Relate to Evangelism?

Approaches to evangelism using the popular "chasm" explanation is a very appropriate tool for communicating with someone that has a history with religion, believes in God, and believes in heaven. To this person, the need to connect with God through accepting Christ's sacrifice and turning from sin makes sense once explained.

However, for many of the people in our two camps, this explains what Christians believe but doesn't compel them to action. The chasm of sin doesn't readily play a part in their chosen spiritual path. If the God sitting on the other side of the chasm looks anything like organized religion or Christianity as they know it, they have no desire to cross. The answer to the question "How

do I get to God?" is irrelevant to them. The new question is "How do I become a better person?"

To bridge the gap, we must dig deeper into the psyche of the lost. The more we understand about what needs and motive drive humanity, the better equipped we will be to help them on their journey toward truth.

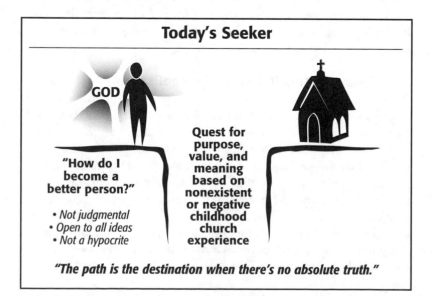

Needs and Motives

As humans we constantly seek to address our needs and wants, but no matter what we accomplish, there always seems to be something missing. Plato addressed this in his "Moral Psychology." Sheldon Wein, of Saint Mary's University explained it quite well: "Human beings come to have certain wants, and reason tells them how to satisfy them. Yet working at satisfying the desires one happens to have will not necessarily maximize satisfaction, because our true natures are such that each of us has a basic and powerful passion for fulfillment. This desire, the desire for fulfillment, is one of which most people are unaware. Satisfying the wants we happen to have is not, as a matter of contingent psychological fact, a good, or efficient, means of satisfying the fundamental desire for fulfillment, which we all possess."[5]

The quest to find fulfillment begins primarily at the door of love, acceptance, and belonging. In relation to God, self-esteem is a result of where we receive our value, never fully realizing our potential until we align our purpose with God's idea of where we should go and who we should be. It is critical to understand what is common to all humanity and how it relates to our relationship with God. After all, we are on a journey to help people in their quest for spiritual completeness. The need for love, acceptance, and belonging undergird the driving motivations for all of humanity. Before applying that knowledge to evangelism, let's take a look at a biblical interpretation.

Desire to Be Known

The Bible has quite a bit to say about the drive of humanity for love, acceptance, and belonging. Through the stories of average people, God's Word demonstrates the value these individuals placed on being known. And Christ's insight into who these people really were and what they really needed forever changed them.

The story of the woman at the well in the book of John, chapter 4, is often used as a perfect example of effective evangelism because it gives the perspective of both the seeker (the woman) and the evangelist (Christ). The story begins with a seemingly casual conversation. The great life change occurs when Christ reveals knowledge of her true heart.

16 "Go and get your husband," Jesus told her.
17 "I don't have a husband," the woman replied.
Jesus said, "You're right! You don't have a husband – 18 for you have had five husbands, and you aren't even married to the man you're living with now." 19 "Sir," the woman said, "you must be a prophet."
28 The woman left her water jar beside the well and went back to the village and told everyone, 29 "Come and meet a man who told me everything I ever did! Can this be the Messiah?" 30 So the people came streaming from the village to see him.
39 Many Samaritans from the village believed in Jesus because the woman had said, "He told me everything I ever did!" 40 When they came out to see him, they begged him to stay at their village. So he stayed for two days, 41 long enough for many of them to hear his message and believe. 42 Then they said to the woman, "Now we believe because we have heard him ourselves, not just because of what you told us. He is indeed the Savior of the world." (NLT)

How does the woman react to being known so fully and without judgment? Her response was to believe in Christ's deity and to trust in his words. She could not conceal her joy and amazement at being truly known. Although speaking with Christ revealed her sins, he did not shame her but rather gave her hope and freedom from her wretched, empty life. See, the value she placed on being known and accepted was greater than the pain of hiding her sins. Freedom comes when light shines in the darkness.

Every human desires to be known. But unless you are able to see into people's lives like Christ could, how can you help the unbelievers God brings your way to have their need to be known met? You have to get them to tell you! The rub is that they aren't likely to tell you unless they feel safe and have a high degree of certainty that you will not reject them.

Grace Is the Key
Understanding the non-Christian is about understanding all humanity, but also grasping the one difference that separates all believers and nonbelievers. Being fulfilled, rooted in acceptance and love, is a need of all people; but nobody understands the power of

grace until they've experienced it. To experience that acceptance, you have to truly be known, because your fulfillment goes only as deep as the knowledge that acceptance is based upon. God created that desire in us, for God alone to fulfill. Our life's pursuit to find fulfillment elsewhere will always be incomplete because God is the only one who can truly know us better than we can communicate (Col. 2:9-10).

What they need is grace, but that is precisely the one thing that they cannot understand. Theological grace is defined as "The divine favor toward man; the mercy of God, as distinguished from His justice; also, any benefits His mercy imparts; divine love or pardon; a state of acceptance with God; enjoyment of the divine favor."[6] Makes you feel all warm and happy inside, doesn't it? Hardly!

You cannot truly grasp the magnitude of the grace and power of God and the Holy Spirit intellectually, anymore than you can understand the warmth of a summer day by watching TV. You can know all the facts of heat transference, sunburn, and the human nervous system, but it can't be personally real until it impacts the individual. It is experiential, as much as intellectual. You can get close to understanding when someone describes his or her own experience, but your experience would be unique for all the same reasons that you are a unique person. Hearing someone else describe that experience should merely create a greater desire in yourself to make it your own.

Luke 12:6-7

"Are not five sparrows sold for two pennies? Yet not one of them is forgotten by God. Indeed, the very hairs of your head are all numbered. Don't be afraid; you are worth more than many sparrows."

Until we find our value through acceptance by God, we mask our true selves. It is the reason for chasing of pleasures, quests for wealth and influence, and attempts at personal improvement to make knowing us desirable. Also, it is why many of us choose to be alone for fear of our true selves being discovered and rejected.

Christ is no longer physically here to speak face to face with the lost and do miracles to prove His deity and caring heart, but you are. He did the most wondrous miracle in saving you from your own sin, and he gave you his Spirit to guide you and teach you and lead others to salvation through you. People need to be known, but fear rejection. They need to see a miracle to know that God is alive. Your story of grace—the impact of God in your life— is that miracle. Your desire to honestly know them and care for them regardless of their sin, is the introduction to grace they need to feel safe in pursuit of God. The telling of your story is the first step to learning theirs.

I argued facts and history with Jim, and we both lost. As soon as I challenged his belief, he switched on defense mode. Because he saw me as an aggressor, he was blinded to any grace I attempted to communicate. I got it backward, and it was a very difficult lesson to learn. *Showing* Jim Christ *before* I earned the right to tell him about Christ was where I missed the mark. At that time my passion for evangelism was not purely driven from the source of God's passion. Once I discovered how God felt about Jim, my approach to everyone I encountered took a dramatic turn.

---

1 www.Sputnik7.com
Radical Beauty Concept (independent video)
director(s): Nick Philip
studio: Sublime Films
country: UK
[1997]

2 Barna Research, "Atheists and Agnostics Infiltrating Christian Churches," October 15, 1999.

3 ibid.

4 Apologetics is a branch of theology devoted to the defense of the divine origin and authority of Christianity.

5 Sheldon Wein, of Saint Mary's University,
http://www.bu.edu/wcp/Papers/Anci/AnciWein.htm

6. theological grace definition, Webster's Revised Unabridged Dictionary, © 1913 MICRA, Inc.

CHAPTER THREE

JESUS GOT IT!

Epiphany Step One—The Purpose of Permission

I stood there, transfixed on the invisible words floating above the room full of curious onlookers. Everything is marketing. Everything is marketing when you are dealing with influencing people's beliefs in a way that encourages them to take action. It was so simple. I've said it a million times. Marketing 101 was really Life 101. Marketing and sales once were different steps along the same path with common purpose, but those lines have blurred considerably over the years. Marketing drives prospects to salespeople when necessary but often closes the deal directly. When we do anything to help set the stage for someone to make a decision—hopefully for his own benefit—we are marketing.

I thought about my own definition of marketing: *The science of leading prospects to take specific actions to fulfill a perceived need or desire.* With the addition of God's Spirit, and the action as accepting Christ, it sounded a whole lot like evangelism.

Every human being in westernized culture succumbs to the influence of marketing to the masses countless times a day, but the church has great difficulty influencing those same people with a more valuable, pertinent, and personal product—salvation. Could the key to reaching our modern society be the integration of the truth of the Bible and the communication principles of modern marketing?

"Michael? Hello? Do we need to take a break?" My assistant prodded me to focus.

Wrestling my thoughts into temporary submission, I pressed on with the meeting, but the question had ignited a brushfire of ideas. I soon called one of my staff to the board to drive the discussion, whipped open my notebook, and hastily transcribed these basic thoughts in hopes of recapturing the moment at the end of the day. My mind was reeling, yet I was focused. Although I had spoken those words a hundred times, this time they took on new meaning. This time they had eternal purpose.

As head of marketing strategy for a large division of a two billion dollar software company, I spent a great deal of time studying and teaching marketing principles. Considering myself a professional student of both marketing and strategy, my book-shelves were crammed with the latest concepts and theories. There is a nugget of useful experience in each encounter with a new author, but the value is unrealized until you mold those theories to the specific needs a company and market demand. That was my job for the last several years.

Through time, I became confident in my ability to synthesize heavy concepts and pull out the applicable component, often merging dissimilar components to suit our needs. This time, though, the specific need had nothing to do with my company. Although my work consumed my days, my obsession was focused elsewhere. I desired purpose in my life, in my work, and in all my relationships. I had been changed by God several years earlier after chasing lies for around thirty years and committed the rest of my days to guiding others in understanding of these same life-changing truths. With the same fervor and energy applied to my profession, I attacked the study of evangelism.

The history of marketing has gone through many cycles and in recent years had experienced dramatic change. Because the Internet now enabled customers to be more informed, have more options, become more in control, marketing was now more responsible for sales instead of just generating leads for salespeople. Interruptions no longer were sufficient because their responsibility now included leading the customer all the way through the buying process. Marketing had a lesson to learn. Many in the industry finally figured out what successful salespeople learned decades earlier: trust was critical to building the most important objective of customer inter-action—a meaningful relationship.

Relationships built on trust and honesty were the keys to repeat customers, and more importantly, communication about needs and desires. Once customers know you understand and appreciate their situation and who they are, they will put up with a lot of mistakes. You will also have earned the right to challenge them to act, and they become willing to be challenged.

Evangelism is marketing in this sense, more so than passing on information. When I speak of selling and marketing metaphorically to evangelism, I am talking about building a relationship, based on trust, which leads to helping that potential "buyer" fulfill a need they have identified. This is not about being an insincere used car salesman. If using the words "sales" and "marketing" make you uncomfortable in the context of evangelism, we have something in common. Marketing people are equally unhappy with the metaphor. As we move through this topic, hopefully you will see both a little differently.

Our Canvas Is Set

A growing trend in the art world over the last few years has been in mixed media and unique canvasses. I was in an art gallery recently to view the work of an artist who painted atop anything he stumbled upon, as long as it wasn't a standard fabric canvas. The foundation for these gorgeous works of art, from an extremely talented painter, were old doors and windows, roofing from a house, sheet metal, stainless steel, boards, and even wads of paper from the trash. I'm not qualified to be an art critic, but I have recognized that a lot of mixed-media artists compensate for lack of painting skill with creative combinations of elements. They play to their strengths and try not to highlight their weaknesses. There's nothing wrong with that, and I would consider it wise, but even though it may make them good artists, it doesn't necessarily make them good painters.

The mixed-media artist at this gallery was a remarkable painter. So much so, at first I wondered why he chose such difficult materials as the foundation for his work. A proper canvas makes the act of painting considerably easier, and faster; there are less surprises, and the artist is in total control. Then it dawned on me that this artist was so confident in his ability, he reveled in the challenge of *not* being in total control.

When using materials such as metal, wood, or glass for a canvas, you must treat them all differently. Some surfaces do not allow paint to quickly set, so you must wait considerable lengths of time before applying other colors. Some paint will simply run and is thus useless, forcing you to adjust the mixture, time, heaviness, and layers to suit your conditions.

As Christians we must accept the condition of our canvas, work with it, not against it, so we can eventually transform the surface to accept our thoughts, ideas, and words. (Of course, our thoughts, ideas, and words must be an accurate communication of the truth of Christ or they will still fail.) Just like that creative and determined artist, we must be patient, yet purposeful; we must be accepting, but not complacent. The negative perception that exists of Christians in America and most westernized countries is the hand you are dealt. Don't bemoan it; seek to understand and make the most of it. Grab your brush and go to work. After all, even DaVinci painted the Mona Lisa upon a simple piece of wood.

Connecting My Experience with Evangelism

Even after I had accepted this canvas and attempted to work with it through study and practice to become proficient at evangelism, I still experienced great resistance and spectacular failures for many years. In my quest for wisdom and skill, something was still missing after years of studying apologetics (defined as defending the Christian faith), faithfully attending seminars and classes, being involved in missions, traveling across the country to attend theological debates, and visiting with renowned apologists and teachers. I had even taught several classes on evangelism, yet still experienced as much awkwardness as success when sharing my faith.

Having actively shared my beliefs since accepting Christ in 1992, I seemed more comfortable than most of the Christians I knew who cowered at the mere thought of talking about Jesus in the workplace, with their friends, or to their family. Others, it seemed, rarely saw fruit from their conversations, but felt obedient and even triumphant because they had merely carried out their perceived *duty* of delivering what they had learned in a class. Some seemed to have less concern for the impact on the person they were speaking with than the fact that they fulfilled an obligation. Evangelical legalism, it seemed, was as prevalent in the modern church as evangelical timidity.

With so many resources available to us, what was the problem? Something had to be wrong. God desired us to serve with joy, but there didn't seem to be a lot of glad hearts concerning this perceived burden to "Go and make disciples" (Matt. 28:19). Was it the resources, the motivation, or something else? With all my experience and training, why did I still find myself in just as many conversations that ended poorly as ended positively? Better still, why was that a great batting average? We weren't playing baseball, here; we were dealing with the eternity of my friends and family!

That day of epiphany in the conference room began a dramatic change in my life and in my relationship with God. God calls us to be as "wise as a serpent but harmless as a dove" (Matt. 10:16, NLT), and it was time for me to get wise. I spent my professional career searching out any possible angle to reach my potential consumer, but limited my efforts in evangelism to listening to Christian teachers. Don't get me wrong, the theologians and pastors I encountered were brilliant, learned, and had answers, important ones. But the competition, Satan, working through the world and the popular media, seemed to be winning.

The competition of modern western culture used every effective marketing method available to capture attention, drive people to action, and often unwittingly, away from God. They were relentless, and at first glance to the consumer, had a more compelling product. Perceived wisdom, affection, and power were the emotional tools of the trade. Salvation, on the other hand, requires relinquishing control to an invisible God, acceptance of personal weakness, and on-your-knees humility. It's not an easy sell and impossible to get results without God's leading. It is also rarely a quick response in a postmodern society that hardly understands the basics of the Christian faith.

God had me in marketing for a reason. Should I ignore what I learned in business, or can God use everything we learn in life to reach the lost? The answer had to be yes, as long as it didn't contradict biblical truth. I set out in hopeful pursuit of defining this connection and testing my newfound hypothesis.

It worked. From that day forward I tailored my approach to these new ideas, my heart experienced a grand transformation, and lives of nonbelievers changed around me every week. As I shared my newfound insight with other Christians, they began to have similar experiences. I based this book on the course developed from those insights and how God led me and my students to more effectively reach a generation that is seeking spirituality but rejects the traditional church.

Epiphany Step Two—The Missing Link of Permission

After the epiphany in the meeting, I began to go back to many of the recent marketing books that helped mold my own successes in reaching the corporate consumer. Parallels of sales and marketing to evangelism abounded once I looked through the right filter to connect them. After all, as crass as it sounds, I was a "salesman for salvation." Christians didn't create the product of salvation by grace, as salespeople don't normally create the products they sell. But by extolling its benefits, tapping into the natural need of the prospective consumer—humanity, we help lead them to a positive decision.

One particular book entitled *Permission Marketing*, by Seth Godin, pioneer of modern direct and Internet marketing, struck a strong chord. When I read the words through this newfound filter (words in parenthesis are modified), the excitement built.

> Permission (Evangelism) lets you turn strangers, folks who might otherwise ignore your unsolicited offer, into people willing to pay attention when your message arrives in an expected, appreciated way.[1]
>
> Imagine your (evangelism) message being (listened to) by more than 70 percent of the prospects ... Then imagine that more than 35 percent respond. That's what happens when you interact with your prospects one at a time, with individual messages, exchanged with their permission over time.[2]
>
> [Permission Evangelism] cuts through the clutter and allows (a believer) to speak to prospects as friends, not strangers. This personalized, anticipated, frequent, and relevant communication has infinitely more impact than a random message displayed in a random place at a random moment.[3]

When I reread those words, I was inspired to dig deeper. I desired to no longer share the promise of salvation with strangers, leaving them as strangers, but to bridge the gap of trust that would lead them to listen and trust my words. In addition, I wanted to figure out who was a good prospect before I whipped my personal testimony out of the holster. It's the first step in marketing and sales—identify good prospects and focus.

Many times in my life, actually most of my life, when people tried to evangelize me, it caused more harm than good. Many of the scars I carried through my life that kept me away from seeking truth in God were delivered at the hands of well-meaning Christians. They had no idea who I was or what I was seeking, but they interrupted me and tried to force their beliefs down my throat. I've never bought a product that way, and I sure wasn't apt to buy God that way. If going to church subjected me to hundreds of those kinds of people, I definitely wasn't headed there. Like much of today's society, I chose not to become assumptive and insensitive, so I incorrectly chose not to be a Christian.

The very next day after I accepted Christ, I prayed that God would never allow me to forget what it was like to live a life without knowing Him. I asked for the emotions and experiences to remain present with me so that I could always relate to non-Christians, forever remaining empathetic. I have prayed that prayer numerous times in my life, and God has always honored that request. Now I was given the insight to use the heart God had provided to be as effective as possible. It is exciting to use the methods of the world to reach the world, yet see eternal results.

The purpose of permission in evangelism is to create trust, get around the legal and social barriers to discussing your faith, and most importantly, to discern the leading of the Holy Spirit in someone's life. The result is fruitful conversations, more often, and the ability to speak with confidence in every encounter. Evangelism, when *asked* to tell someone about Jesus, is easy and resembles giving an answer for the hope that you have, rather than forcing an answer on a person yet to ask a question. Permission is biblical, and Jesus' example bears witness that it not only is God-inspired, but effective.

Mark 10:17-23

As Jesus started on his way, a man ran up to him and fell on his knees before him. "Good teacher," he asked, "what must I do to inherit eternal life?"

"Why do you call me good?" Jesus answered. "No one is good—except God alone. You know the commandments: 'Do not murder, do not commit adultery, do not steal, do not give false testimony, do not defraud, honor your father and mother.'"

"Teacher," he declared, "all these I have kept since I was a boy."

Jesus looked at him and loved him. "One thing you lack," he said. "Go, sell everything you have and give to the poor, and you will have treasure in heaven. Then come, follow me."

At this the man's face fell. He went away sad, because he had great wealth.

Jesus looked around and said to his disciples, "How hard it is for the rich to enter the kingdom of God!"

Do you think Christ gave up too soon? Shouldn't he have encouraged the man instead of pointing out his difficulty? Why didn't Jesus stop him? Surely, Christ was capable of convincing him that the treasures of this life are no match for the joy he would receive for following God.

Jesus could have given the young man insight into the vision he had for the growth of the church starting from these simple beginnings and the part the man could play in that. He could have described in detail the joys of being in relationship with God and asked other disciples to give personal testimony as to why they made that decision. He could have used the old standards of guilt, shame and fear, extolling the agony of hell, or even telling the young man that if he walked away his story would be told for thousands of years, as a bad example.

Of all the people in all of time who could have been great at sales, Christ should have been the best. After all, nothing was beyond him. He should have never lost a sale. In sales terms, the young man was a great prospect. He was pre-qualified, having shown up to the event, listened intently, and expressed interest in the offering of eternal life. He was already further along than most of the disciples, so his struggles with sin might have been easier, making him more effective right from the beginning (I'm speaking logically and earthly here, not biblically). This man also might bring a great deal to the ministry including funds and the influence of political and religious leaders, maybe taking some pressure off in the local community.

These reasons are pretty logical and reasonable, and sound similar to many that I hear when people, including pastors, describe someone they are excited to evangelize. Christ was evangelizing, but it sure doesn't look like the way most people do it today. Even though it says Jesus loved him, he stood there and let the man walk away. Why did Christ not follow him when he walked away? Why didn't he try harder when this man seemed so eager? Why didn't Jesus "get him saved" before addressing this difficult area of his life?

Christ picked the one area of the young man's life that he knew would be the hardest to forsake. He called the man to uncompromising commitment. When it was time to make a decision, Christ allowed him to choose wrong and walk away. Jesus knew that until the young man could relinquish that one area of his life, he would not be able to accept the message of grace. Christ also knew that this scene would be played out in other lives again and again. He let it happen. Was the man's choice Christ's personal failure—an indication that he had not tried hard enough, hadn't said the right thing, or had given up too soon? "Jesus looked around and said to his disciples, 'How hard it is for the rich to enter the kingdom of God!'" Jesus cooperated with his Father's drawing work and didn't try to force the issue.

Christ's approach was first to weed out the *willing* seekers and then go deeper with them. He promised hope over pain. He condemned sin, not the sinner. He never attacked; he invited. Love is a choice, so it can never be forced and genuine at the same time. Salvation is choosing the ultimate expression of love and adheres to the same rules. Christ's approach is based on his equal desire for love and his respect for the gift of free will. When looking for a spouse, one woos. Threats are never the basis for a healthy relationship.

What Jesus Knew

What did Jesus know that we are missing? Jesus knew when to talk and when to walk. Was his style so different because he was God, or can we learn from what Jesus did and define a new approach of our own? The answer is obvious, but it is undeniably hard to translate into personal action unless we understand Christ's point of view and apply it to real life situations.

When Jesus Christ spoke in the synagogues, where the audience was well versed in Jewish Law and the text of Scripture, he taught straight from Scripture. He used the Law to shine the light of truth on the hearts of his listeners. For the last year or so of his ministry, he left the synagogues and taught in homes, fields, and along the seashore. He still quoted Scripture, but he used miracles to gather people to him, he told parables to sift out the hard-hearted, and he taught scriptural truths by making connections to life.

Gather, Sift, Teach—Jesus' Threefold Approach

Initially, people came to see the miracles, and word would spread in a matter of minutes that Jesus, the Miracle Worker, was in town. At times these occasions probably had a carnival-like atmosphere. This seemingly normal guy shows up, with masses of people following him, and miraculous things start occurring. Everyone starts buzzing about how he healed the blind town beggar or made the lame man—you know, the one you passed in the market just yester-day—walk. Why, they are even whispering stories about him raising the dead! How could you not drop everything you were doing to check it out?

Imagine it: huge numbers of people crowding around to see the miracles. Everyone is quiet while the blind man stands before Jesus and states his request. Murmurs and whispers from the back, heads turning in question and puzzlement, an occasional out-burst—a cheer or sneer. As the man steps back and opens his eyes, you could hear a pin drop while everyone awaits the verdict. Uproars of cheers rise as word travels through the crowd. "I can see!" shouts the man, and then a sudden rush as others in the crowd press forward to present their child, their brother, their friend. To some it was a sideshow—a novelty of sorts—meant to entertain them and nothing more. But to others it was clear that something incredible and true was occurring, and this man, this Jesus, had the touch of God.

In the second phase of Jesus' approach, the dynamics dramati-cally changed. Jesus talked to them in parables, confusing stories that required considerable effort to process. The teeming crowd began to thin as those who had come merely for the show were forced to think. No doubt many walked away thinking, "Fun's over. This guy speaks in senseless riddles. I gotta get back to work." The group that remained, possibly much smaller than the original, willingly struggled with the imagery, desperately seeking the answer.

What separated those that remained from those that walked away? They had witnessed the same miraculous demonstrations, but the response of their hearts was different. Some had selfishly (key word) sought only entertainment and to be a part of the latest "happening," while others saw the same miracles and sought truth. They stayed because they wondered if *their* lives could be changed by this man from God. They likely grouped up, offered theories as to the meaning, asked questions of the disciples, and hung on every word of Christ.

Jesus understood that most of these people would not understand his parables. Think of it. His disciples didn't even understand most of the time. After telling the parable of the sower, Matthew tells us that the disciples collectively came to Christ and asked him "Why do you speak to the people in parables?" (Matt. 13:10). In his response, Jesus addresses their concern for the crowds, even though the disciples probably wondered at their own lack of understanding.

[11]He replied, "The knowledge of the secrets of the kingdom of heaven has been given to you, but not to them. [12] Whoever has will be given more, and he will have an abundance. Whoever does not have, even what he has will be taken from him. [13]This is why I speak to them in parables:

"Though seeing, they do not see;

though hearing, they do not hear or understand. [14]In them is fulfilled the prophecy of Isaiah:

" 'You will be ever hearing but never understanding;

you will be ever seeing but never perceiving.

[15] For this people's heart has become calloused;

they hardly hear with their ears,

and they have closed their eyes.

Otherwise they might see with their eyes,

hear with their ears,

understand with their hearts

and turn, and I would heal them.'"

Jesus told parables to sift the crowd, separating out the hard-hearted from those who had the heart to understand. He didn't tell parables because ALL people were deaf to them. He told parables to separate those seeking truth in God and willing to make the effort from the carnival goers with selfish hearts. I also think it is somewhat humorous how Christ responds to his disciples.

> 16"But blessed are your eyes because they see, and your ears because they hear. 17 For I tell you the truth, many prophets and righteous men longed to see what you see but did not see it, and to hear what you hear but did not hear it.
> 18"Listen then to what the parable of the sower means"

Jesus first tells them that their eyes and ears are blessed because of what they see and hear (his miracles and parables); assures them that many prophets and righteous men longed for this same experience, but were denied (so they should be grateful), and then explains the parable. Obviously, his disciples didn't get the riddle either. Jesus saw through their question, presented as concern for the other followers, as equal concern for themselves. They wanted to know the answer too! Yet he didn't shame them because they didn't get it. Instead, he honors their search by telling them that parables are a gift and vitally important. Then he explains the meaning of it in simple terms.

Like the twelve, those who survived the sifting of the parables remained to hear the deeper teachings of Christ. They were the earnest seekers—the open hearts drawn by the evidence of God's Spirit in Jesus (as demonstrated by his miracles). Everyone was eager to see the miracles, fewer made it through the parables, and still fewer presumably sat through Scripture teaching. Those with hearts prepared to hear and discern truth, leading to a personal response in action (Matt. 13:15, *"turn, and I would heal them."*), were the blessed ones, the ones with eternally changed lives.

Christ didn't run after the rich young ruler because he knew the young man's heart wasn't ready. Jesus knew and let him walk. Jesus never ran after anyone. Instead, he made himself available to those willing to wholeheartedly seek the Way to God, the Truth about God, and the Life found in God.

What Jesus' Miracles Tell Us about Evangelism
Mark 10:46-52

> Then they came to Jericho. As Jesus and his disciples, together with a large crowd, were leaving the city, a blind man, Bartimaeus (that is, the Son of Timaeus), was sitting by the roadside begging. When he heard that it was Jesus of Nazareth, he began to shout, "Jesus, Son of David, have mercy on me!"
>
> Many rebuked him and told him to be quiet, but he shouted all the more, "Son of David, have mercy on me!"
>
> Jesus stopped and said, "Call him." So they called to the blind man, "Cheer up! On your feet! He's calling you." Throwing his cloak aside, he jumped to his feet and came to Jesus.
>
> "What do you want me to do for you?" Jesus asked him.
>
> The blind man said, "Rabbi, I want to see."
>
> "Go," said Jesus, "your faith has healed you." Immediately he received his sight and followed Jesus along the road.

Besides the carnival-like drawing power of these demonstrations, there is a pattern in the miracles of Jesus that may point us to another one of his guidelines for evangelism. The story of Bartimaeus' healing is a wonderful miracle. There is no doubt it changed Bartimaeus' life forever. It may have even changed the hearts of many of those privileged enough to be witnesses. But as I studied the other miracles recorded in the four gospels, I saw an interesting pattern emerge.

The gospel writers recorded thirty-seven miracles Jesus performed. Out of those thirty-seven, twenty-seven were detailed individual healings like Bartamaeus, with one mention of numerous non-descript healings (Mark 1:32-34). It is likely that these twenty-seven occurrences are just a few of all the miracles Christ performed during his earthly ministry and that they were recorded for our benefit. We can assume, however, that they are indicative of the rest, or under God's inspiration more would have been revealed.

Investigating the twenty-seven recorded healings Christ performed reveals an incredible pattern. With only two exceptions, every miraculous healing of an individual was used either as a specific teaching tool (often to incite the anger of the religious leaders), or it was a response to a direct request. In other words, they had to ask. [For a detailed explanation of the two exceptions mentioned, see appendix A.]

In every other of Christ's twenty-one recorded healings, the person needing to be healed, or someone acting on that person's behalf because he or she was incapable, asked. These individuals received Christ's healing touch after they expressed their need. Here's a quick rundown of some of the most obvious examples:

> Then one of the synagogue rulers, named Jarius, came there. Seeing Jesus, he fell at his feet and pleaded earnestly with him, "My little daughter is dying. Please come and put your hands on her so that she will be healed and live." (Mark 5:22-23)

> The leper begged Jesus on his knees and said "Lord, if you are willing, you can make me clean". (Luke 5:12-16)

> That evening after sunset the people brought to Jesus all the sick and demon-possessed. The whole town (of Capernaum) gathered at the door, and Jesus healed many who had varying diseases. (Mark 1:32-34)

> When Jesus had entered Capernaum, a centurion came to him, asking for help. "Lord," he said, "my servant lies at home paralyzed and in terrible suffering." (Matt. 8:5-13)

> There some people brought to him a man who was deaf and could hardly talk, and they begged him to place his hand on the man. (Mark 7:31-37)

> They came to Bethsaida, and some people brought a blind man and begged Jesus to touch him. (Mark 8:22-26)

> As he was going into a village ten men who had leprosy met him. They stood at a distance and called out in a loud voice, "Jesus, Master, have pity on us!" (Luke 17:11-19)

> When this man heard that Jesus had arrived in Galilee from Judea, he went to him and begged him to come and heal his son, who was close to death. (John 4:46-54)

> In fact, as soon as she heard about him, a woman whose little daughter was possessed by an evil spirit came and fell at his feet. The woman was a Greek, born in Syrian Phoenicia. She begged Jesus to drive the demon out of her daughter. (Mark 7:24-30)

When a miracle involved demon-possessed people, either someone brought them to Jesus or the demons themselves called out to Jesus. This particular woman was told by Christ to wait until he was done teaching his disciples, but she humbled herself and begged even more (Mark 7:27-30).

Even though some people requested, Jesus still required them to spell out that they had faith in his power.

As Jesus went on from there, two blind men followed him, calling out, "Have mercy on us, Son of David!"

When he had gone indoors, the blind men came to him, and he asked them, "Do you believe that I am able to do this?"

"Yes, Lord," they replied. (Matt. 9:27-28)

Again, in the story of Bartimaeus, Jesus even required a specific request when one was not given, even though the affliction and need were obvious.

Throwing his cloak aside, he jumped to his feet and came to Jesus.

"What do you want me to do for you?" Jesus asked him.

The blind man said, "Rabbi, I want to see." (Mark 10:50-51)

Think about it! A blind man is screaming at the top of his lungs pleading for Jesus to have mercy on him. He has no idea exactly where Jesus is so he's frantically yelling in the general direction of the crowd. Maybe his eyes are closed, covered, or even visibly cloudy or disfigured. When Christ stops and the blind man hears that he has asked to see him, the man is giddy with excitement. He tosses aside his cloak (perhaps not the wisest thing for a blind person to do in a crowd) and runs across the street. "Where is he? Where is Jesus? Take me to him!" he screams, anxiously pushing through the crowd.

Have you ever seen a blind man hurrying through a crowd? I'm pretty certain that Jesus knew the man was blind. Still Jesus asked him, "What do you want me to do for you?" (v. 51a). Christ knew, but he still made him ask.

In another instance, Jesus reached out to a conspicuously desperate man. He asked others about the man's condition. "When

Jesus saw him lying there and learned that he had been in this condition for a long time, he asked him, '*Do you want to get well?*'" (John 5:6, italics added)." Jesus asked the question everyone knew the answer to so that the man could confess with his own mouth his need. Why?

I don't think these examples are a coincidence. Nor have I cobbled together Scripture just to prove my point. Christ walked past hundreds and thousands of people who needed healing in the short three years of his active ministry. He knew the affliction over every person in every crowd. Yet Jesus did not indiscriminately heal everyone he passed by waving his hand as he walked down the road—creating a sweeping cure for every ailment. He could have, but he didn't. Why?

The pattern is clear, but the reason might not be as easy to see. These people, or a loved one on their behalf that knew their heart's desire even if they could not express it, stepped out and asked. By admitting their need, their hearts were placed in a willing and humble state. By bringing their request to Jesus, they were acting out of faith.

Humility of this kind is required for salvation and provides a picture of the type of person whose heart is ready to receive Christ. But it also provides us with a picture of a true seeker ready to engage in the journey to salvation. It is evidence of a sincere desire to seek truth, to seek healing of some sort—a need for answers to life's questions and a hope that this man, Jesus, has the answers.

The Way to God

How does a seeker get to God? In order for anyone to accept Christ, experience forgiveness of sins, and receive the Holy Spirit, a miracle of the grandest design must unfold. Once a seeker admits he has a need for healing, he is drawn to God by the Holy Spirit. He must recognize the deity of Christ (or Christ's death on the cross could not atone for his sins). When confronted with the story of grace, the seeker must then choose to confess and repent of his sins and embrace the grace of God freely offered to him or walk away.

Again, Christ is our model for the salvation process. Christ was both fully God and fully man. To grasp how this affects the salvation process, we must dig into the reasons why Christ came to earth in the first place. Of course, Christ came to live a sinless life, die on the cross for our sins, and rise again providing the opportunity for the eternal salvation of mankind for the glory of God. But why did he come as a man? He came to show us his deity—he came to show us God. It seems odd that God would choose to be a man to demonstrate his deity, but he did. Once we understand the big picture, we see it as the perfect plan and the only way it could have worked. The question is, do we see how it works through the believer today?

Christ proved his deity through his miracles, healings, and even his teaching, described as "from God" (John 5:19) and inspired. When he left, his disciples carried on facilitating miracles empowered by the Spirit of God. Just as in the Old and New Testament, demonstrations of God's power draw the lost to repentance and salvation. Salvation requires belief in Christ's perfect deity. Since Christ isn't here to demonstrate his deity with miracles, where are the miracles that woo the seeker today?

Today's Miracles

Demonstrations of Christ's deity and the Holy Spirit are the key factors in reaching the lost, and both require Christians. As believers, we are the manifestation of Christ's Spirit on earth, and he draws the lost to us for either conviction or understanding grace, or both. If miracles are the proof of Christ's deity, and the nonbeliever must believe Christ is God to attain salvation, we must be involved in miracles when evangelizing. We must make the connection.

Great, you say, not only am I responsible for evangelism, but now I'm responsible for doing miracles? Well, not exactly. You should be asking what part you play in demonstrating the deity of God, not how you can personally *do* miracles.

Salvation is the one miracle that merits the rejoicing of the angels in heaven, and they have a party every time it occurs.

"In the same way, I tell you, there is rejoicing in the presence of the angels of God over one sinner who repents."(Luke 15:10)

Guess what, you are the byproduct of Christ's biggest miracle! You are the evidence that Christ is alive today and still changing lives. The Holy Spirit in you is the result of that miracle, and it is there to help you and be a testament to every person who has yet to meet Christ. Let me repeat that: The Spirit in *you* is the miracle that proves Christ's deity, death and resurrection. YOU are the connection!

The Perfect Partnership—The Holy Spirit, the Christian, and the Lost

Christ knows that if someone's heart is prepared to hear truth and they come into the presence of God through his Spirit, they repent and turn to God. Christ desires salvation for every person, so why didn't he stay here and live as God on earth through every generation so that he could meet and influence everyone?

He did.

> "And I will ask the Father, and he will give you another Counselor to be with you forever—the Spirit of truth. The world cannot accept him, because it neither sees him nor knows him. But you know him, for he lives with you and will be in you. I will not leave you as orphans; I will come to you. Before long, the world will not see me anymore, but you will see me. Because I live, you also will live. On that day you will realize that I am in my Father, and you are in me, and I am in you." (John 14:16-20)

We are one with God and Christ through the Holy Spirit, who is with us forever. The Holy Spirit guides the believer and is forever with him.

> "All this I have spoken while still with you. But the Counselor, the Holy Spirit, whom the Father will send in my name, will teach you all things and will remind you of everything I have said to you." (John 14:25-26)

The Holy Spirit convicts the lost, guiding them to their need for God.

> "But I tell you the truth: It is for your good that I am going away. Unless I go away, the Counselor will not come to you; but if I go, I will send him to you. When he comes, he will convict the world of guilt in regard to sin and righteousness and judgment:" (John 16:7-8)

Why did Paul tell the Ephesians, "For you were once darkness, but now you are light in the Lord" (Eph. 5:8)? God's Spirit (in us) exposes sin.

Have nothing to do with the fruitless deeds of darkness, but rather expose them. For it is shameful even to mention what the disobedient do in secret. But everything exposed by the light becomes visible, for it is light that makes everything visible.
(Eph. 5:11-14)

John 3:17-21

"For God did not send the Son into the world to judge the world, but that the world might be saved through him. He who believes in him is not judged; he who does not believe has been judged already, because he has not believed in the name of the only begotten Son of God. This is the judgment, that the Light has come into the world, and men loved the darkness rather than the Light, for their deeds were evil. For everyone who does evil hates the Light, and does not come to the Light for fear that his deeds will be exposed. But he who practices the truth comes to the Light, so that his deeds may be manifested as having been wrought in God." (NASB)

There are only two responses to exposure in the light: repentance or death. God's Spirit in the believer is the convicting force in the world. Conviction leads to repentance and salvation for those seeking truth. Conviction without grace breeds anger, depression, guilt, and resentment. This is one of the principle problems with those claiming to be changed by grace but unable to give it or receive it from others. But conviction is not at all negative when the light you shine on someone's sin simultaneously lights his or her path to freedom from that oppression.

When Christ said he left his Spirit here to guide us, and teach us, and be with us for all time, it was not just for believers. That would be selfish. As an unbeliever, you just get the conviction part first. Conviction humbles you to the point of abandoning the prideful barriers to truth and can lead to repentance with the healing peace given to every believer through salvation in Christ.

2 Corinthians 7:9-10

I now rejoice, not that you were made sorrowful, but that you were made sorrowful to the point of repentance; for you were made sorrowful according to the will of God, so that you might not suffer loss in anything through us. For the sorrow that is according to the will of God produces a repentance without regret, leading to salvation, but the sorrow of the world produces death. (NASB)

Christ is still performing miracles today. The act of salvation: when anyone accepts Christ, experiences the forgiveness of sins, and receives the Holy Spirit, is certainly a miracle of the grandest design. Therefore, like the early disciples, we can walk side-by-side with Christ's Spirit and watch his miracles unfold before our very eyes when we participate with God in reaching the lost.

The simple act of talking to someone about Jesus can be the precursor to an incredible miracle that you are privileged to witness and help facilitate! Although God sometimes chooses to bring someone into his family without a believer being involved, in most cases it is the Holy Spirit drawing them by manifesting the deity of Christ in the miraculous changed life of the believer that leads to salvation.

God has chosen people to reach people. Christ came as a common man to show us God. After 2000 years, God's methods for drawing the lost to himself haven't changed. He demonstrates his deity by way of miracles (your salvation), draws the open hearts that are honestly seeking truth (his Spirit in you), and shows them grace (God's work in you).

This design is not one of necessity for God. He doesn't include us because he is short-handed or lacks resources or means for accomplishing his work. Allowing us to participate in the process is his gift to us.

As your understanding of the impact of God's grace in your own life grows, learning how to communicate that to the unbeliever is paramount. Grace is what changes people. Seeing the result of it in others is what draws people to seek grace for themselves. Your story of grace is the miracle that will change lives.

You may not be able to change the public's perception of the church, but you can change an individual's perspective on how a personal experience with God can miraculously heal and empower, delivering the gift of hope to that person. The best news is that God draws the lost to his Spirit in you. It is not your responsibility to chase them down, try to convince them when they don't want to be convinced, or feel bad when they turn away. We must make ourselves available (which requires deliberately being in the company of nonbelievers) and seek God's Spirit. We need to learn *when to talk and when to walk*, just like Christ.

---

1. Seth Godin, Permission Marketing, Simon and Schuster, Copyright 1999, pg. 50.

2. ibid, pg. 43.

3. ibid, pg. 49.

CHAPTER FOUR

SCARED AND FEELING GUILTY

If you are distressed by anything external, the pain is not due to the thing itself, but to your estimate of it; and this you have the power to revoke at any moment.

—*Marcus Aurelius Antoninus* (A.D. *121* – A.D. *180*)

You gain strength, courage, and confidence by every experience in which you really stop to look fear in the face. ... You must do the thing you think you cannot do.

—*Ellen Roosevelt*

It was 7:00 P.M., and after a very long and busy day, conversation became casual around the office. Samantha, the official office Christian, stood in my doorway anxiously fidgeting as she spoke. She was a faithful believer and seemed to constantly attend church. So much so, that we all wondered how she ever had time for anything else. She rarely socialized in the office, so the fact she was even talking to me, as well as the awkwardness with which she attempted to guide the conversation told me she had an agenda. I had guessed her intentions and lie in wait, prepared to pounce.

This was years before I began actively pursuing truth and answers about God, when my Christian antagonism had reached a fever pitch. I relished the idea of engaging in conversation with "blind-faith Christians" as I termed all members of Bible-believing organized religion. They were always such easy targets to embarrass. Samantha, like most others I came across, seemed to have the cards stacked against her. She had experienced the power of God in her life and desired me to know the same, but walked into battle unarmed. She believed the Bible completely but had never questioned why she did and had no idea how to communicate the positive impact of God in her life. She was a sitting duck that decided to waddle over and visit the nice guy in the camouflage with the shotgun.

The obvious result of such a pairing predictably ensued. After a short time with me posing several challenges, she left my office in tears, I believe, questioning her own faith. I felt victorious! Another brain restored to its rightful home. The attitude of my heart at that time now appalls me, but it was where I stood. I wonder if she ever gained the guts to talk to anyone about Jesus again.

I might have even accepted her faith in the Bible if she had at least been able to express what God had done for her and her husband in a way that didn't sound like they just traded one vice for another. Whether she felt this or not, my impression was that she was a scared woman who felt no safety in her beliefs, no power in the Almighty, and didn't really desire to know me and respect my journey. She was on a mission to tell me about Jesus, for many right reasons, but not the ones that I would respond to.

Today I respect her boldness and resolve, but she had business to do with God before she was prepared to do business with me. She was simply doing her duty as she saw it and may have genuinely cared about me, but she didn't effectively communicate that or even God's care for her. Either might have intrigued me; or maybe nothing would have. She should have determined one of those three choices before pressuring me with the need to accept Christ.

To most Christians, I was one scary dude. As a nonbeliever, I was considerably more aggressive than most of society, but that made me easier to argue with if you were prepared, but few were. Most of these unprepared, well-intentioned Christians were handed their heads, and likely hesitant to ever open their mouths again. Samantha never made another attempt with me, and her misguided approach to a frontal attack merely strengthened my resolve to disrespect Christians.

Like Sheep to the Wolves

You may have run into someone like the pre-Christian me, or at least have heard of such disastrous encounters and envisioned your own personal drubbing. If so, you are not alone. Many Christians are flat scared to stand up and be counted as someone who believes differently. Many more lack the confidence or understanding to defend their belief.

We live in a society that is openly hostile toward anything Christian. Perhaps previous attempts at sharing your faith have led to rejection, damaged relationships, and possibly doubting your own faith. You may also fear cultural rejection, legal ramifications, and missed opportunities in your career. You may justify your silence with reasonable excuses from "If I lose my job I won't be able to tithe" to "If I talk to my friend about Jesus I'll alienate her, so I prefer to let the way I live my life speak for me."

Why don't more believers share their faith? The current social context of distrust, fear, anger, and misunderstanding concerning Christianity has dramatically impacted the view Christians have of themselves, as well as skewing their perception of the desires and power of God. This religious climate has created a profound impact on the freedom Christians once felt for speaking their minds, expressing their faith, caring for strangers, and reaching out to their friends. We realize God desires us to be bold and step out—that we are called to love and acceptance—but it is very difficult to translate that into action when we fear humiliation or rejection.

A Common Problem

It is confusing—this mix of fear and guilt—and has led many in the body of Christ to respond to the chastisement and ridicule of the world much as a child would. Some lash out in anger, picking fights with "sinners" and fueling the fire, others retreat and huddle together with those of like mind, and the rest try desperately to fit in. All of these examples are forsaking some aspect of their relationship with God, and it is the Christian that is missing out. To be direct, *any Christian that is not experiencing regular non-Christian interaction and is not often sharing the reasons for the hope that he or she has is limiting his or her personal experience with God.* It is quite easy to be sympathetic to such frustrations.

An Evening with Ellen

Eight years, working ten feet away, and Paul never knew what Ellen believed and to my knowledge, not once had a conversation about Jesus with her. That was a sobering discovery that I've since found all too common. He was the CEO and founder of the corporation, a faithful and public Christian figure in the business community, and she was his loyal executive assistant. They knew intimate details of each other's lives, yet that knowledge was compartmentalized and ultimately unimportant in the grand scheme of life, because none of it seemed to have much eternal significance.

I started at the company less than two weeks earlier to run worldwide marketing. Ellen worked just down the hall and was instrumental in helping me get settled until I hired my own assistant. One evening we were both working late and she came in to check on me. Being after regular work hours, as is so often the case in the business world, it is easy to drop the walls of hierarchical appropriateness and engage in more meaningful conversation. I broke the ice by asking her a few questions such as why she worked for the company and how she first met her boss.

As expected, she responded in kind and asked me why I came to Arizona, a question I would get hundreds of times while living there. My response surprised her, but led her to ask a series of questions that ultimately let me know she was interested in spirituality and even hearing about Jesus Christ. The conversation was a perfect example of the permission process that we will discuss in detail later, but the important thing to know now is that in only a few minutes, two relative strangers were deep into a conversation about their beliefs, within the safe environment created by my vulnerability and her invitation.

The day after that first conversation I was so excited to tell my Christian CEO, her boss, about the encounter and gather any info he had about her spiritual journey to help me better reach her, that I almost tripped over myself as I ran into his office. I relayed the events of the evening and stood expectantly to get his side of the story. What surprised me was that he had no information to share. He was shocked on more than one level that the conversation even occurred.

He seemed envious about my conversation but attributed it to me being "gifted" in this area, never expecting similar results for himself. Although he was encouraging, he also cautioned me to not "go too far" and to "be careful" that I did not alienate others. Many of his concerns were logically valid but actually unnecessary. His primary issues echoed the top three typical push-backs I receive in my courses when encouraging evangelism at work:

- legal ramifications
- creating work tension
- damaging your reputation

Ignorance of the legal way to accomplish this is the excuse most people use for why they don't, but the real reason has very little to do with the law. [The Civil Rights Act of 1964 does not prevent proselytizing or sharing your faith if done properly.] The concern for creating work tension by appearing pushy and contentious, and damaging your reputation, making it difficult to properly interact with your coworkers, is valid, and I think completely justified.

It is justified because telling someone about Jesus when they have not invited you into that conversation is almost always inappropriate and wrong. It is wrong at work, and it is wrong in other areas of your life.

I believe my friend Paul had a heart for lost people because, although he had concerns, he was genuinely excited about my conversations around the office. He also believed that because he was the boss, it was inappropriate to cross that line. However, after getting to know him and understanding his position with God, I believe he had the perfect job.

Paul thought the reason these conversations happened was because of me, not because of what I allowed God to do. He thought he simply wasn't an evangelist.

I'm No Evangelist

At the opening of every evangelism workshop I've taught, I ask how many people accepted Christ before eighteen, and invariably, over 90 percent of the room raises their hands. Once, in a room of about sixty people from a very mission-focused church, there was only one who was an adult convert. With less and less adult converts in our churches, the majority of those responsible for connecting with the present adult culture accepted Christ as children.

They never lived a life totally separated from God. Most never even stepped away from their faith for any extended period of time. They think this is precisely the reason why they are ineffective, and I think that's sad. To believe that you are comparatively inadequate to reach the lost because you've spent too much time in relationship with God is the most discouraging statement I can imagine. Of course, they never say it in such a concise statement, because when you hear it expressed that plainly, it sounds almost silly.

Childhood converts do have some valid reasons for their awkwardness and reservations because, among other things, they feel they have nothing in common with nonbelievers and fear they have no compelling story. Based on this, they conclude they can't be evangelists, and no wonder. Given all the requirements and perceived issues people associate with being an effective evangelist, they're right. It isn't practical for most people. But, could it be that most Christians know more about reaching the lost than they think? Is it possible that the best evangelists in the world aren't eloquent speakers, don't have theological degrees, and don't even necessarily know how to be good at connecting with the unchurched?

I submit that the general public perception of who is fit to be an evangelist is more than a little skewed, thus the picture we have in our heads makes it quite difficult to imagine ourselves in that role. What we have to reconcile is that God saw all of us in the role of contributing to the salvation process of the people he puts in our paths and expects us to eagerly embrace that responsibility. Therefore, something must be amiss with our expectations of fulfilling what we are called to do, or God misspoke. I won't even justify the latter by addressing it, because we must assume as Christians that God and faux pas can't coexist.

Aside from the handful of gifted Billy Graham-like orators that arrive every couple of generations, the most effective evangelists actually number in the hundreds of thousands but should number in the hundreds of millions. "So," you say, "where are they?"

Look in the mirror.

Does that sound too trite to justify consideration? Standing alone, in its current condition, I readily admit that statement is quite the pat answer, but bear with me. The reason why you may reject that idea is exactly one of the central issues we must address.

Even after hearing all the arguments about common men and women from the New Testament being used by God to reach thousands, it probably still seems too otherworldly to believe that could happen to you. It just isn't practical, is it?

"I'm not a good speaker."

"The times were different then."

"I don't know enough."

"I have to provide for my family; I can't give everything away and go do missions. I have a career."

"Being Christian isn't new and different anymore, it seems old and irrelevant to my friends."

"I will get in trouble at work."

To make it a little easier to swallow, that you too could be used by God in dramatic ways to reach hundreds or thousands in your lifetime, consider the adult convert that experienced radical life transformation after accepting Christ. We've probably all met at least one person miraculously delivered from extreme anger, depression, illness, crime, or addiction, who is compelled to extol the amazing power of God in his or her life. Consequently, that type of person is usually the most effective evangelist in your church. These people usually speak freely to anyone without fear. They are invited to present their story in front of church congregations and outdoor festivals, and often end up starting ministries for people still caught up in the sins they've since abandoned.

They are also, unfortunately, too often the bane of the childhood-converted Christians' existence. They are one of the primary excuses I hear at my workshops for being poor at evangelism. "I don't have a story like that person. I don't have a radical transformation. I accepted God as a child and never did any of that stuff. Well, except for that first year at college, but after that ..."

The Power and Pain of Guilt

Why do so many Christians feel guilt and regret about evangelism? Do you feel guilt when you are worshiping God? You may on occasion because of something God is trying to work on in your life. But do you allow it to stop you from ever worshiping again? The test to determine whether what you are hearing is from God or not is if there is an action due on your part.

God-centered worship, and that includes evangelism, does not lead to guilt unless God is trying to exact a change (repentance) in you (2 Cor. 7:10). That kind of conviction is the result of your connection with the Holy Spirit leading you to remove barriers to your closeness with God. Therefore, if your past experiences with evangelism created a sense of guilt, either that guilt was not from God or something about how you evangelize isn't honoring to God. If so, you absolutely must discover what that is, confess it to God, and turn from it.

There's nothing like the zeal of a new convert to shame a life-long Christian. Have you ever analyzed why the brand new convert is often so effective at reaching the lost? Even if they are occasionally clumsy and scripturally ignorant, they seem to always have a list as long as your leg of people they have spoken to about God during the previous week. They monopolize the prayer request time at the weekly Bible study.

As wrong as we all know this is, for many of us, their enthusiasm is quite annoying. That is because their enthusiasm is convicting. These people can make you feel guilty about your own evangelistic efforts, or lack thereof. In comparison, although we logically accept that it isn't a competition, we feel disobedient to God. We respect them, but secretly wish they would just disappear.

I can relate because I was this person and saw the impact first-hand. After the initial weeks of my very first men's Bible study, the rolling eyes at prayer request time became obvious and I felt the tension whenever I spoke. One of my friends directly confessed his disdain for my enthusiasm, but even though he didn't blame me, I became disturbed and cautious when hit with the reality that I was different. Both of us felt guilty, but only one of us should have.

My friend's guilt led him to repentance and eventually into a more active role in the lives of the people God brought into his life. His response was correct. My response was not. I cut my prayer request list each week and spoke a little less enthusiastically about my interactions with nonbelievers. My enthusiasm for evangelism waned, and I became one of the holy huddle, engrossed in church functions and biblical learning, all the while sharing my faith with diminishing enthusiasm and results.

I was a new Christian and desperately wanted to fit into my adoptive family. I found that being an enthusiastic evangelist in an American church filled with childhood converts made me quite different indeed. Thankfully, it was merely a short-lived cycle, and I was back to normal in due time, knocking over scores of china with every turn of my new Christian bullhorns. I was rather clumsy in my evangelism attempts, but after that initial lapse, my enthusiasm blinded me to anything that would deter my efforts.

God even used my Bible study and those same friends to pull me out of my evangelistic funk. I'm not sure if my friend ever was aware I went through that cycle or his role in its beginning and ending, but as our relationship deepened, he and the other men helped me recognize and appreciate the differences in each of us and how God uses them. As one of the godliest men I have ever known, his heart wasn't misaligned or out of step with God, he simply had to unlearn his definition of evangelism. That experience is one of the many that led to this book. He truly desired my enthusiasm for sharing with the lost, and experiencing it first hand shined a light on his life resulting in *holy guilt*. Unlike the guilt I experienced, his was just what the doctor ordered.

Many Christians feel guilty about evangelism, either because they don't do it, do it poorly, or just don't care. If you suffer from envy, anger, or guilt regarding anyone that is more effective than you at reaching the lost, you must determine where that feeling is coming from and what you need to do about it. They could be shining light on a dark area of your life that you must turn over to God (Rom. 2:17-23).

Why They Can and I Can't

When faced with the evangelistic zeal of an adult convert, don't ignore them—analyze them. The reason more adult converts enthusiastically share their faith is because many have the complete package of necessary components for effective evangelism. Simply put, they are overwhelmed by the love of God and amazed at how he has worked in their life. That's the most important piece; but if they also couple that with social awareness and respect for another person's journey, you have someone that is highly effective at doing God's work. That is the complete package. It bears repeating.

The effective evangelist is:
- Overwhelmed by the impact of God in his life
- Respectful of another person's journey

Does it sound too simple? Consider this; in my experience, during the first year after conversion, the adult convert on average will talk to more nonbelievers about his faith than in the following five years. Why? Because I believe that most people know more about evangelism in the first year after accepting Christ than after they've become "educated" and "mature" Christians. Even more disturbing is that, in my experience, the average new Christian no longer has a single significant relationship with a nonbeliever after just a couple of years."

It is also true that the changes that occur in that first year are very noticeable to everyone close to the new Christian. The change in lifestyle or attitude demands questions, and evangelism opportunities are born of his or her responses. The new Christian's hope in Christ is the reason for the change, and he or she must be prepared to answer the onslaught of inquiries.

> But in your hearts set apart Christ as Lord. Always be prepared to give an answer to everyone who asks you to give the reason for the hope that you have. But do this with gentleness and respect ...
> (1 Peter 3:15)

Unfortunately, as we mature as Christians, our hope often becomes less obvious. Shouldn't it be the other way around? Don't you think our hope in Christ would increase with our experience with Christ? If not, something is missing, and usually it is a clear understanding of the impact of God in your life.

As a brand new Christian, it is easy to compare yesterday to today. As a child convert, yesterday seems too far away to relate with our present experience. As a mature Christian, we usually prioritize our non-Christian relationships around church outreach activities instead of the other way around. Churches should not only teach their mature Christians how to reach others, but as soon as possible, they need to educate the "emboldened by recent conversion" Christian. They are highly effective and usually need to know much less than the mature Christian to feel confident.

Of course, that confidence can also be dangerous, and it is not uncommon to encounter the bull-in-a-china-shop Christian who is so enthusiastic about his personal experience he repels everyone. He charges out of the gates of conversion swinging a hardback Bible at everything in sight. He believes that if people simply hear what happened in his life, they would be compelled to make the exact same decision. He is dumb-founded when the response is repeatedly cold or hostile, and soon finds himself in a holy huddle with other disconcerted, would-be evangelists, developing a personal relationship with God with those of like mind, and nobody else.

The initial enthusiasm is laudable, but coupled with insensitivity and not backed up with considerable thought and prayer, the results are frustrating and confusing for everyone involved. Zeal for obedience and compassion for the lost doesn't mean one should lose respect for the people you are trying to reach. Although I counsel and seek to redirect the efforts of these eager young Christians, I love their hearts. They are uncalculating, willing to risk all, and it is refreshing if not always effective.

Evangelism Is Not a Duty

The typical Christian sees evangelism as a deed to be done out of obedience to God rather than an aspect of their relationship with God that is greatly enhanced when partnering with him. We are told to evangelize because it is our "duty" as a Christian. The call to guilt-motivated, proclamation evangelism is very one-sided, and hardly motivating. We are told to "win the lost to Christ." I detest that phrase. Love is not a contest. Sure, we are in battle with Satan, but that battle is the Lord's. We are soldiers, not generals. We are to do what we are told and trust our general. That does not mean to go fight any battle we see fit. That means that when we are in battle with our full support structure, we can be confident in victory of the war, regardless of what the battle looks like.

Our general has chosen the right foe, the right battle field, the correct armament, and the perfectly trained and prepared troops, of varying skills and abilities, to accomplish the task at hand. We are not mercenaries. We are not snipers working alone from a distance. We are battling Satan as a soldier in God's army using every element GOD PROVIDES to vanquish the foe.

God provides everything we need. We have all the elements for success if we can learn to identify and use them:

- Evidence of Christ's greatest miracle
- Proof of God's power and love
- God's heart for the lost
- The Holy Spirit to guide the lost to us and direct our conversation

Every Christian has all of these necessary elements already, but those that have difficulty sharing their faith are living with one or all of the following barriers:

- They don't understand how to relate to today's seeker.
- They can't articulate the work of God's grace in their own lives.
- They don't share God's passion for the lost.
- They don't know how to respect each individual's unique journey.

Have you ever asked yourself WHY you believe the Bible? Why do you follow Jesus? Why do you care if anyone else does? Why do you have hope in Christ? What has He ever done for you? What would your life be like without God?

If you can't answer these questions, it will show, and you will soon be exposed. The truth must be evident in your personal experience and your heart before it can touch the heart of another. Until Christians understand the answers to these questions, the church in western culture will remain stagnant. Evangelism efforts and training that do not first answer the personal questions of the evangelist are doomed to failure. If you don't understand the grace you have received, how can you help someone else see the value it provides?

It's All about Grace

Most churches make it easy for Christians to slink into group solitude and continue to lick their wounds long after they're healed. The current culture in many churches focuses on building an internal community. Community has its benefits for personal and corporate growth, but it rarely involves injecting the members into the community around them except during special events. Despite these attempts at service to God and community, the Christian is becoming increasingly distant from popular culture, thus making it difficult for those living in that culture to relate or desire to engage in conversation. Do any of the following statements reflect your thoughts?

- "I need to know more before I can be a good evangelist."
- "I don't have a story that could reach anyone. I've been a Christian since childhood."
- "I don't have anything in common with adult non-Christians. I'd be better off trying to connect with children."
- "I'm not as smart as some of the people I know at work; I would just embarrass myself. Some of the more zealous, angry, anti-religious people even seem to know the Bible better than I do."
- "I haven't found the right method of evangelism. I hope this book is the solution."

If you can relate with any of these questions, you may believe that your own salvation is purely by grace, but you might be shying away from evangelism by accepting too much of the responsibility for the salvation of others. Do you believe that your mistakes, inexperience, or lack of knowledge can prevent someone from gaining the "gift" of eternal life? Do you believe that your actions or inadequacies can derail someone's heart and steer them out of relationship with God? Do you believe that your works can lead to someone's salvation?

If a person's works cannot lead to his salvation, why should your works lead to his salvation?

Okay, I know I'm twisting you up a bit here, but this is a vitally important perspective to grasp. Am I advocating doing nothing? Is it wrong for you to study and learn how to be a better evangelist? No, that would contradict biblical truth since God calls followers of Jesus Christ to spread the promise of salvation to the lost and calls us to be wise in our dealings.

Evangelism is not a duty, or a task we take on to assist God. We rarely will successfully share our faith out of responsibility. Sharing your faith out of duty will never lead to the success that sharing your faith out of love and amazement at God does.

For the church to effectively reach the unchurched requires an unlearning of methods for fulfilling the "duty" of evangelism and an intellectual retrogression resurrecting our amazement at the miraculous gift of grace. In short, we must return to simple delight in the Lord and respectful sorrow for the lost. When we are amazed again at the work of God in our own lives, we cease to suppress the Holy Spirit. When the Holy Spirit is free and evident in our lives, God draws people to us. Then, and only then, will we be effective in evangelism.

Christian Cop-Outs

It was the saddest attempt at evangelism I have ever heard, yet the woman on the radio was so proud, so happy, and encouraged because her experience was at the center of a radio marketing spot. The organization behind the ad promotes buying new testaments and giving them away as gifts. Great idea, huh? I thought so, at first. That is until I discovered that the gift of a Bible was the only act of sharing your faith that they promoted. They called it "The shy person's evangelism."

The experience the woman was so excited about occurred when she finished a long cab ride. After paying the cabbie, she handed him a Bible and said, "I have a gift for you." The driver said thank you and took the Bible. Evidently, these were the only words spoken during the whole cab ride. She was excited about that? I just shook my head and changed the station.

This isn't at all a slam on the distribution of Bibles, as I see that as a noble and worthy pursuit. The Gideon's, for example, have touched many a lost soul by making God's word available in hotels and motels throughout the world. I, myself, had even turned to one of those nightstand beacons of hope when lonely, desperate and unaware of God's love. So, what's the problem?

I use this example to make the point that choosing a single act of evangelism as the one thing you are to do, unless God has specifically called you to do that in an individual situation, is probably not sufficient. It could be just an escape from the very action God desires you to take. What I am warning against is the lie that evangelism can be limited to something impersonal and void of risk. I call this *Hit and Run Evangelism*, and it allows neither the evangelist nor the nonbeliever to garner maximum benefit from the experience. Is your choice of evangelism completely safe? Is it easy? Does it require you to rely on God? Are you growing closer to God through doing it, or does it just make you feel good about yourself?

Then there is the myth of missions. I love that U.S. churches are among the largest supporters of international Christian missions. I've enjoyed my personal experiences, and every person I've known that has gone abroad has been changed forever. Unfortunately, missions are often used as another cop-out for Christians scared of personal evangelism.

God expects evangelism to permeate every aspect of our lives just like he calls us to constantly pray (1 Thess. 5:17). Most people are not called to forsake everything and commit themselves to foreign missions, but we are all called to be actively involved in the salvation of others. If mission support or involvement is all you are doing, though, ask yourself this: Do you support Christian missions abroad to fulfill your responsibility to reach the lost? Are you giving to missions because you are afraid of stepping out in faith yourself?

The Three C's

Effective evangelism requires compassion, consideration, and the great Counselor. In other words, you must have the heart of God for the lost, think about and understand their needs and the best approach, and allow the Holy Spirit to guide your conversation and prayers for the person God has directed your way. When done with every element in place, the results are remarkable. So much so, evangelism can be a little selfish in an okay way. It can become completely intoxicating to be used by God in such a way, and desiring that is not wrong. It's almost hedonistic sometimes!

"My most intense spiritual pain is when I find myself drawn to those things that repel God and repelled by those things that draw Him. My most satisfying spiritual pleasure is when I find myself drawn to those things that draw God and repelled by those things that repel Him. I want to be attuned to God's heart, to be of one mind, one spirit, one disposition with Him." [1]

Sharing your faith can be the most rewarding experience of your life on earth. There is nothing that so honors God and puts the Christian more in the hands of faith and obedience as building a relationship with a nonbeliever on a journey for truth. All you need to get started is a compassionate desire born from God, and a person to engage in conversation. You must consider both as gifts from God and not happy coincidences. The ability to discern the ready heart, open to receiving your message, is impossible without the Holy Spirit active within you, but your heart must first be willing to awaken God's desire. Until your heart is filled with awe for what God has done in your life, you can never reflect God's heart, and he will likely not honor you with the blessing of spiritual conversations even if you are actively engaging non-Christians.

The greatest joy in your life may just be a conversation away. In fact, it may just be ten feet to your left. Lift your head out of this book for a minute and look around. Who do you see? Who do you see every day? They see you and probably know something about you is different. You can bridge that gap on their terms, but you must be purposeful. You must try. Look what you could be missing.

---

1 Sam Storms, « Pleasures Evermore, » pg. 106, NavPress, 2000.

CHAPTER FIVE

GETTING PERMISSION

Colossians 4: 5-6
Be wise in the way you act toward outsiders; make the most of every opportunity. Let your conversation be always full of grace, seasoned with salt, so that you may know how to answer everyone.

1 Peter 3:15
But in your hearts set apart Christ as Lord. Always be prepared to give an answer to everyone who asks you to give the reason for the hope that you have. But do this with gentleness and respect ...

Continuing My Conversation with Ellen:

"So, what made you want to work for a software company in Phoenix?" she casually asked, expecting to hear the standard "career advancement" and "seeking a new business challenge" mumbo jumbo.

I replied, "Well, I am on the board of a nonprofit organization that is based here, and for a while I have been thinking about moving to become more involved. This company seemed like a good fit and allowed me to do just that."

"That's interesting, what's the nonprofit?"

"It's an organization that helps people understand spiritual perspectives on social issues using the arts. We do events of all sizes using poetry, video, open discussion, and some pretty eclectic musical artists. It's a lot of fun, and very thought provoking."

I silently prayed for God to reveal the path this conversation should take, and rather suddenly, it appeared.

She was intrigued and appeared more than a little surprised. "That's interesting, how did you get involved in that?"

"Spiritual things didn't interest me much for most of my life, then about nine years ago, my perspective completely changed. Seven years later, I got involved with these folks."

I left that statement hanging in the air, resisting the urge to blast out my testimony.

Silence.

I allowed it to continue and fuel the already pregnant pause. I kept thinking about the movie *Braveheart* and the scene where Mel Gibson as the Scotsman, William Wallace, leads his men on foot into an unbalanced battle with the English on horseback. His men knew all too well that in 300 years, no Scottish infantry had ever defeated the cavalry. Their only hope was to surprise the attackers at the very last moment by raising twenty-foot spears just as the enemy horses were at full charge. Anxious and afraid, Wallace's men's eyes dart back and forth from the galloping horses to him, as he repeatedly yells, "HOLD, HOLD, HOOOOLLLLLD!" At just the right moment, with the cavalry in full stride barely a second away, Wallace screams "NOW!" Spears are raised and the battle is in full play with Wallace's men at a sudden advantage.

Ellen was not my enemy, but I would be fighting her fears and false impressions of Christians. Satan is my enemy, and I knew he was lurking, hoping to create doubt and fuel any fear Ellen might have. Timing was critical, and maybe the only reason for the picture in my head. I held, and waited for the Spirit to draw the cavalry to me. Ellen paused, and sat down indicating she wanted more of the story.

"So what happened nine years ago?"

My eyes darted to William Wallace, and my heart to God. I was certain that this was the moment, but the Spirit replied:

"HOLLLLLLLD!"

I prayed silently and responded, "It might sound kind of weird, but I once was considered an atheist by most people's definition until something happened to change my mind. I was challenged to really pursue spiritual truth, and I discovered that my perspective on God was completely wrong."

I still didn't give it all to her just yet. If God was leading her to hear about him, I knew we would get there. I didn't need to rush.

"What happened that changed your mind?"

William Wallace stared directly at me and once again bellowed, "HOLD!"

"It's kind of personal, but I'm happy to share it with you if you really want to know."

"Yeah, I'd like to hear, that is, if you don't mind. Are you a Christian?"

"What do you mean by Christian?"

Well, that set her back on her heels. She didn't know quite how to respond, not knowing exactly where I stood, but did her best. With her simple reply, I was able to determine her basic understanding of Christianity and her personal feelings toward people who profess to be Christians. She seemed to understand many of the basics of Christian belief but also appeared wary of organized religion because of her experience with hypocrisy.

This was invaluable information, considering she had just given me permission to tell her my testimony. I was able to agree at some level with her feelings, making a very personal connection before delivering my story in a way that demonstrated both the similarities in our lives and God's work of grace.

The conversation naturally eased into her invitation to me, "So, what do you believe about God now? What changed in you?"

This was the moment God had planned; my obedience to the Holy Spirit had taken our conversation exactly where God intended it to go. In only a few minutes, two relative strangers were deep into a conversation about their beliefs, within the safe environment created by my vulnerability and respect for her journey, as well as her subsequent trust and invitation. As I outlined my conversion process and shared the subsequent changed life, I allowed her to guide the conversation by cherry-picking the issues where she connected. I didn't have to guess. We had created an environment of questions and answers that was quite comfortable, and because the Holy Spirit had prepared her heart to seek spiritual answers, she gladly continued that process. As our conversation hit its stride, I was able to ask a question similar to the one she had asked me,

"What do you believe about God?" and the conversation shifted from my story to hers by connecting on our common ground.

I have no idea how long we talked, but I know it was quite late. I'd love to say that she accepted Christ that night, but it was clear that she still had a lot to consider. What she did do, though, was take a book I just *happened to have* in my office that allowed her to reason through her objections on her own. We were often both at the office, late at night, so we continued the conversation several times throughout the next month. This culminated in her attending a nearby church on Easter, where she remained committed a year later, and she began living a very changed life.

That incredible evening began with a casual question I would be asked hundreds of times while living in Phoenix. I had carefully planned my open-ended response so that it did more than deliver the asked-for information—it invited her to ask a series of questions. The questions she asked showed me she was interested in spirituality and open to hearing about Jesus Christ. This progression was not by chance, nor was it manipulative. That open-ended question provided an opportunity I knew I would receive many times, so I planned my response beforehand. This example demonstrates how a Permission Evangelism conversation uses responses to simple, superficial questions or statements to help you determine the movement of the Holy Spirit in the life of a stranger. With a little prayerful and purposeful planning, this technique prepares you to give an answer for the hope that is in you using everyday conversation openers.

Down to the Basics

Let's make this really simple. In its most basic form, what happens in an evangelistic encounter? Initially, your goal in a conversation about God is to help bring a person to the point of *acknowledging his need* for salvation, *increasing his understanding* of God's desire for relationship, and *presenting the means* by which he can experience that relationship. Remember, all you can do is provide information about the most important and personal decision people will ever make; the rest is up to them and God. But for this to be a fruitful conversation, you need to require information from them, and they must receive information from you that merits action on their part. What you are initially "selling" is trust.

In chapter one, we talked about how today a person's most valued commodity is time. You are asking someone to commit time to listen, ask questions, possibly read, and think. You are asking someone to face and reveal his or her personal feelings, doubts, fears, needs, and struggles to you. That kind of vulnerability is risky. Normal people won't release this information without some perceived benefit that outweighs the perceived risk. *Throughout your conversation, you must ask yourself the question that is on their minds: What's in it for them?*

The "heart of permission is giving the stranger a reason to pay attention."[1] You must offer some promise of return, or incentive, for their investment or they will never engage the process. That incentive must be "overt, obvious and clearly delivered."[2] Simple curiosity will take them a step or two down that path, but the promise of changed life, as demonstrated in your own grace story, will be quite compelling if their heart is prepared. The combination of curiosity and an interest in the promise of spiritual fulfillment is evidence of the Holy Spirit pulling them along.

People seeking truth will remain engaged as long as the source of the answers is a trusted source. By creating a meaningful, personal dialogue, you are building a relationship, even if you are only with an individual for a few minutes. By being vulnerable enough to share the most meaningful experience of your life—your conversion story—in a very personal way, you are building trust.

The Effective Evangelist

Evangelism is both dangerous and practical. We risk socially and relationally in our obedience to God, but we should be diligent with our intent and efforts. In Matthew 13, Christ identified the many possible responses of hearing the good news of salvation in the parable of the sower.

"A farmer went out to sow his seed. As he was scattering the seed, some fell along the path, and the birds came and ate it up. Some fell on rocky places, where it did not have much soil. It sprang up quickly, because the soil was shallow. But when the sun came up, the plants were scorched, and they withered because they had no root. Other

84

seed fell among thorns, which grew up and choked the plants. Still
other seed fell on good soil, where it produced a crop—a hundred,
sixty or thirty times what was sown. He who has ears, let him hear."
(vv. 3-9)

Most often when we read these words we are tempted to see
them as a matter of fact assessment of the way things are, which is
disturbing. We also are taught these verses in context of defining
the role of the church in nourishing and growing new believers,
but that assessment, although in part correct, is incomplete. Christ
didn't call this the "parable of the *seed*," but rather the "parable of
the *sower*," so we should also see it as instruction to the evangelist.

"Listen then to what the parable of the sower means: When anyone
hears the message about the kingdom and does not understand it, the
evil one comes and snatches away what was sown in his heart. This is
the seed sown along the path. The one who received the seed that fell
on rocky places is the man who hears the word and at once receives it
with joy. But since he has no root, he lasts only a short time. When
trouble or persecution comes because of the word, he quickly falls
away. The one who received the seed that fell among the thorns is the
man who hears the word, but the worries of this life and the deceitful-
ness of wealth choke it, making it unfruitful. But the one who
received the seed that fell on good soil is the man who hears the word
and understands it. He produces a crop, yielding a hundred, sixty or
thirty times what was sown." (vv. 18-23)

I spent my summers as a youth working on my uncle's farm. It
was 200 acres of some of the prettiest bottom land you'll ever see,
with the cool waters of the Soquee River running right through it,
perfect for giant fields of green beans and corn, and even a few
small patches of squash, zucchini, and strawberries. No matter what
we grew, I always loved the corn most. There's just something
about a mile straight of row after row of seven-foot-high green
stalks blowing in the wind.

If you were involved in the months of planting, coaxing, and
nourishing those fields, it would take your breath away. As a sower
of spiritual seeds, a flourishing crop has similar impact. As a farmer,
or sower of seeds, why would you sow your seed on a busy path,

toss them in rocks, or scatter them in a thicket? Wouldn't you always want to use only the good soil? You have to pay attention to the condition of the soil.

Farming in modern times is very different than 2000 years ago, but the principles and impacts of planting will always apply. Seed is planted primarily in the furrowed, nourished, and softened soil—soil that has been prepared—otherwise, you are wasting your seed. Scattered seed will still sometimes sprout and grow—it may even bear fruit. But the harvest is so much more plentiful when the seed is planted in soil that has been prepared.

A few weeks after planting time, I remember seeing small corn stalks showing up wherever a seed tractor had traveled during planting. The more experienced the driver, the more fruitful and accurate his planting, but traveling to and fro about the fields, seeds were bound to drop en route.

Those seeds would sometimes produce corn or beans, but because the plants grew up outside the clean, organized rows, we couldn't use the machinery to harvest it. Usually those plants would just die, unless we made the effort to pick some of them by hand, depending on how much time we were spending with the good crop. You see, as a farmer you have limited time to accomplish your job. There is a great sense of urgency, and your priority must be where the harvest is most fruitful.

I wish we all felt an equal sense of urgency regarding evangelism. I wish we could get a good grip on the need for economy of our efforts. God's salvation is a free and unlimited offer to the world. But as his evangelists, we do have limits. Harvest time is at hand. And we are looking at soil that is largely unprepared. The first disciples had the prophets, and a great majority of the people they were trying to reach regularly attended synagogue. Harvesting was focused on showing how the Scripture they believed and studied daily was fulfilled in Christ. Unfortunately, we no longer have the social foundation of biblical truth to start with. Today we have equal, if not greater, need for sowers as well as harvesters. In this time, we can often be involved in both.

Our time is limited, so we must guard against tossing our seed about willy-nilly. We must feel an urgency to till the soil with our love, building relationships with the unbelievers God brings into our lives. And we must be prepared to place our seed in the good soil—whether made ready by us or by others—so that the harvest will be full.

Finding Good Soil

How do we identify good soil? Not everybody is interested in hearing about Jesus today, but many are interested in aspects of spirituality and will engage in that conversation at some level. To determine if someone's heart is interested in hearing about Jesus, it is easy to take her through a simple process that is honoring to the seeker and reveals the level of interest in spiritual things.

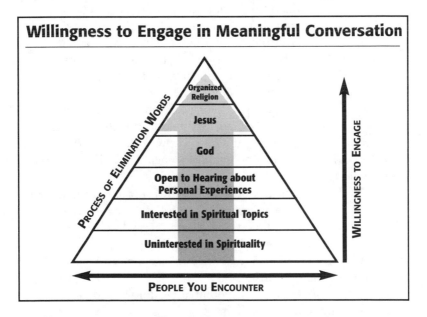

As the graphic demonstrates, you will encounter many more people throughout your days than are willing to engage in conversations about Jesus and even fewer about church. But you will find a great deal of people these days that are interested in spiritual topics. Some of those people prefer only superficial conversation, but others are interested in your story and how your life has been changed. If the conversation makes it that far, it is highly possible that they will invite you to tell your story of salvation. Notice that "organized religion" is the top of the pyramid. This is not because it is the destination for your conversation—just the opposite—in most cases it is the last topic you should approach.

These steps don't always happen in order, but as we move further through the permission process, you'll see how someone's personal interests will play into his or her decision whether or not to engage in spiritual conversation. Don't count on reading someone's face or body language as a way to identify how the Holy Spirit is leading. You may find clues there but some people are better than others at hiding their concerns, desires and emotions.

The Permission Evangelism conversation is much like inviting someone down a long hallway with doors lining both sides. In most cases, you have no way of knowing where the seeker will stop, indicating a doorway into his or her heart. That's why opening many doors of potential conversation is critical to discovering someone's desires. Not all seekers are attracted to the same doors. So often we drag them headlong into the brick wall at the end of the hall, never allowing them to even peak into the rooms en route. We've missed the openings that matter most to those to whom we are talking. If they desire to know you, know truth, or know God, they will find a door, and they will enter, inviting you to come along.

It is also important to note that the lowest level on the graphic represents a seeker with an extremely cynical attitude, often brought about by a childhood hurt. But at every level you can expect some amount of cynicism and skepticism. Just because someone is interested in spiritual topics doesn't mean he is open to organized religion or Christ.

Each level presents both a potential roadblock and an opportunity to continue the discussion.

In the Permission Evangelism conversation, when you allow the non-Christian to move away from topics that are uncomfortable, you leave the door open for him to address those issues with you in the future. In fact, because you approached a topic that made him uncomfortable, *but didn't press*, he is more likely to come to you and initiate discussion in the future. This has happened to me countless times: hours, days, or even months afterward a person will return so that together we can explore that uncomfortable topic.

The key is leaving the seeker with a question unanswered, giving him or her the impression you have the answer, but will not press it upon them. This gives the unbeliever both control and responsibility—that kind of respect and empowering is often missing in other forms of evangelism. Many times I've had someone opt-out of a conversation when I mentioned the words "church," "God," or "Jesus," only to reenter months later when questions brewed in one or all categories. In the meantime, you should "actively wait"—praying, seeking out, and preparing the way into a fellowship of believers—but your biggest responsibility will be to trust God to be working even when you can't see it.

Understanding Permission

Before we jump into putting the process into practice, we must understand a few foundational truths concerning getting permission to talk about Jesus and salvation. As we mentioned earlier, you are "selling" trust, first and foremost. It is important to understand that "trust is not an event."[3] Trust is built through a series of permissions, and although that process can sometimes happen quickly, it always goes through similar steps. "Permission is just a step away from trust."[4] Once someone gives you permission to provide information, and they deem your response valuable or interesting, they will give you more permission.

Throughout this process you will discover who they [the non-Christians] are and what they want. In fact, you may even help them identify what they want in a way they can articulate, possibly for the first time. Remember, "every communication must be crafted with the goal of ensuring that it's not the last one."[5] The best way to do this is to make sure they know *they are in charge* of choosing how much information they receive. They must know *you honor their choices* at their level of willingness to engage, or they will feel pressured and threatened and trust will be broken.

The ultimate goal of Permission Evangelism is to "get them to give you more and more permission over time until they say 'I do.'"[6] That's an apt objective because you are inviting them into a lifetime relationship with Christ, the Bridegroom. This may sound like an odd metaphor because you aren't inviting them into a lifelong commitment with you. To keep your role in proper perspective, remember that they are not necessarily attracted to *you*, but rather God's Spirit in you. Because of our physical presence at work, on the plane, and in the neighborhood, we are God's representatives to the non-Christian—willing conduits to enable the relationship that really matters (between God and the seeker) to grow.

As this conduit, we must be purposeful yet respectful. Permission Evangelism is *responsive*, first to the Holy Spirit in you, and then to the expression of the Holy Spirit guiding others via their questions. Permission Evangelism is *honoring* to God and the seeker. And Permission Evangelism is *challenging* to you and them.

There are a few rules to keep in mind. *"Permission is nontransferable, and it is a process, not a moment."*[7] Just because *you* have received permission, doesn't mean another Christian can walk into that person's life and pick up where you left off. Permission is a personal transaction of trust so every person involved must be willing to invest. Inviting another Christian to participate means they start at ground zero, and that includes clergy. Don't assume that unbelievers will respond better to a pastor, because they may not respect his position and may see him as irrelevant. "Granting permission is also selfishly motivated. If that person ever reaches the point of asking the question 'What's in it for me?' and the answer is 'Not enough!' there is no more value to them to remain engaged, and they will cancel the permission."[8] And remember, if they are in control, they can cancel at anytime.

A Permission Conversation

"What brought you to Phoenix?" It was the question I received from Ellen, and it is a question I still receive years later. There are always questions that we are regularly faced with that could be answered factually and tossed aside as superficial information, or we can use them to determine if someone is interested in spiritual things. That is the first step toward engaging in a discussion about your faith. It answers their common question or addresses a comment, is always open-ended, and always leaves only one or two obvious questions as possible responses.

The interesting thing is over half the people that ask why I moved to Phoenix never ask the obvious question left hanging by my open-ended response. Countless times I've responded with, "I'm involved in a nonprofit organization and found a job that allowed me to move and become more involved," only to have them immediately change the subject. Several times I've had the intention of sharing my faith only to realize by their apparent lack of interest in me as a person that speaking of my faith would certainly have over-stepped boundaries. If they didn't care to know about the most superficial aspects of my life, they surely weren't ready to hear about my salvation. The more I use these types of conversation openers, the more I get in touch with how a person is allowing the Holy Spirit to lead them.

Anticipating opening questions and planning for the best responses became more difficult when I left the corporate world to write this book. You can imagine how repelling it would be to tell someone who isn't a Christian that I was writing a book to teach Christians how to "evangelize" non-Christians so they will turn their lives over to God. The line of folks signing up for that conversation would be pretty short. It took a while to come up with a response that wouldn't immediately end the conversation, but the results were worth the effort.

Now, when someone asks what I do for a living, I say that I am an author. They *always* ask what I write. I tell them I'm working on a new book, and they *always* ask what it is about. After that, I respond that for years I wrote in the technology and corporate arena, but this time my book is more spiritual in nature. Sometimes they opt out immediately. Once, though, I had a total stranger grab a chair, sit down and tell me she was fascinated with spiritual things. Right there in the coffee shop, she began to reveal her personal journey. For ten minutes she dumped her baggage at my feet and allowed me to rifle through it before she even asked more specifics.

Most don't respond so aggressively, but they either ask what I mean by "spiritual" or why I changed direction. If they ask why I changed direction, I tell them that I had an experience ten years ago that gave me a vision for my life, and writing the book was helping to fulfill that vision. I tell them that God led me to teach people to respect the spiritual journey we are all on, and I've been teaching classes that do just that. This book is the result of positive response to those classes. If they ask what I mean by "spiritual," I tell them that my book is about helping people understand their relationship with God in a way that allows them to communicate to others what they believe.

The second time I tried this, I had a woman say, "Why does anyone need a book about that? Don't people know how to do that already?" To which I was able to ask, "Really, what do you believe about God?" In the long discussion that followed, I revealed my story, and as she revealed hers, her inability to concisely articulate her beliefs demonstrated the need for my book. Intrigued (curiosity) and wanting to learn more (because of a perceived value to herself), she asked me for guidance (further permission). We've had conversations since, and her journey for truth has finally begun in earnest.

What? You're not writing a book? What kind of conversation-opener can you use? I am convinced that if you apply prayer and effort to it, God will reveal to you a trigger phrase for your situation. Even if you are in full-time ministry, there are ways to open conversations that are engaging and not repelling. Try describing the results of what you do, instead of branding it with a label. Try something like, "I help people pursue spiritual answers to life's issues." I'm not advocating hiding what you do if someone asks. I'm just suggesting the benefits to help them feel comfortable enough to ask. For help in discovering your own trigger phrases, see appendix B.

Here's another example of a trigger phrase using a statement-based opening instead of a question:

Person at work: "Boy, they were so smashed last night. I don't know how they come to work after a night like that."

Evangelist: "I understand it because I used to do that too, but about ten years ago I had an experience that changed my perspective. Now everything is different. I don't seem to miss it, though."

A statement like that is what I mean by a trigger phrase.

Trigger Phrases and Words

The process of inviting a conversation about spiritual issues initially begins with the interjection of a "trigger phrase" into your conversation. The purpose of the trigger phrase is to get non-Christians to ask a question. Then you expand that permission by revealing more (vulnerability) and interjecting new leading statements. Their questions guide you until they either opt-in or opt-out, telling you exactly how far to go. Using these leading statements and "trigger words," words that will either repel or invite depending on the spiritual readiness of the seeker, you are gradually raising their level of permission until they ultimately ask you to tell your story of salvation.

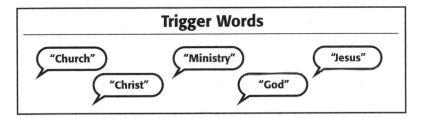

After a trigger phrase, a question will often ensue, and it is your job to allow it to unfold in a way that reveals the nonbeliever's desire for truth. As you saw in the earlier pyramid graphic, it is helpful in every social situation to understand words that trigger decisions about further participation, but it is critical in conversational evangelism. "Trigger words" will either invite or repel depending on someone's background and preconceived notions. These words also help you discern if someone is open to discussing issues of faith. It is important to try not to use words that might alienate the seeker until you can demonstrate that it is safe to talk to you about something as personal as spiritual matters.

Trigger phrases pull a superficial conversation into a personal direction, but without force, so the other person isn't made to feel uncomfortable. A trigger phrase tells the person you are open to revealing a bit of your life if he is curious. It leaves a question hanging between you. If he asks it, you know he cares. If he doesn't care enough about you as a person to ask the question, what makes you think he will be open to you presenting the Gospel? Trigger phrases open the door that leads him toward a point of personal connection where he may or may not give you permission to share your story. Each leading statement intentionally draws them deeper so that you can move to the next step and introduce a trigger word.

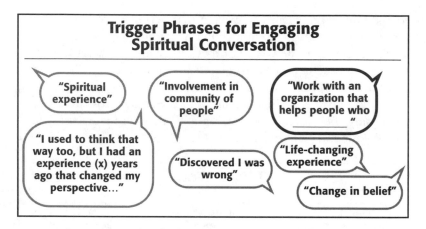

Trigger Phrases for Engaging Spiritual Conversation

"Spiritual experience"

"Involvement in community of people"

"Work with an organization that helps people who ____"

"I used to think that way too, but I had an experience (x) years ago that changed my perspective..."

"Discovered I was wrong"

"Life-changing experience"

"Change in belief"

Remember the hallway of doors analogy? Think of trigger words as doors that progress down the hall toward your goal (sharing your grace story). Together you and the unbeliever work your way down the hall until you use a word that triggers a no-response, or a redirection. If he doesn't ask the obvious question, he is not ready to walk through that door. Let him opt out gracefully and continue your job of active waiting—that means, at the very least, praying for the soil to be prepared and for more opportunities to deepen your relationship.

Wondering if you will ever cross paths with this person again? If this was a short conversation, on a plane for example, try to find some reason to exchange business cards and e-mail addresses. Give the person an opportunity to re-engage the conversation. Drop him a note every few months, even if it is just a funny e-mail, to let him know you are willing to talk. If he never responds, pray for God to bring another sower into his life, and don't give up on him.

If the conversation went several levels deep, and especially if you were invited to share your story before the conversation ended, have confidence that God is working on that person, and you were a link in the chain. Pray for more links, more willing harvesters, and for that person to listen to the leading of the Spirit. You may be surprised one day with a phone call, letter, or e-mail letting you know that your seeker has come to faith. But, then again, you may also never know until you reach heaven.

The Permission Process in Action

As you move through the process, you present opportunities to opt-in or opt-out to determine an individual's willingness to engage in further conversation, all the while giving him an easy exit, but leaving the door open for him to reenter at will.

Here's an example of how I might guide a conversation by introducing a trigger word as part of a leading statement: "My perspective about God changed when I met some pretty incredible people in Atlanta, and I now think differently." Or "It may sound kind of odd, but I had a spiritual experience that changed the direction of my life. Nothing has been the same since." Those statements obviously demand a question: "What has changed?" or "What was so incredible about them?" I wait, but the person often doesn't say a word. If he doesn't ask the obvious question, he is opting-out of the conversation. But don't be surprised to discover that the question stays with him.

Once, months later, out of the blue, someone walked up to me and said, "A while ago you mentioned something about your life changing ten years ago. What was that all about? What changed?" At that point I was given permission to give my testimony, and her salvation process began in earnest as we were able to compare and contrast experiences and draw parallels between her need and her needed solution, namely grace.

What brought her back to her unasked question? During the waiting period, dramatic changes had occurred in her life that made her question her purpose in the world. When she realized she needed to seek some answers, she came to the one person she knew that seemed to have experienced the same questions and found an answer. She could come back—opt back in—because I had allowed her to opt out with grace and had remained approachable.

The purpose of the process is to increase your sensitivity to the urgings of the Holy Spirit in the other person's life. When you find yourself in a conversation where you are pretty certain you should tell someone the Gospel, employ the permission process anyway. If the person refuses to ask the most obvious of questions, without even the slightest religious trigger word from you, because of the process you will understand that it is not God's timing for you to share. In those situations, you'll find yourself standing on the precipice of spilling your spiritual guts, only to discover that the other person doesn't even care about the most superficial side of your life. *What initially appeared as an opportunity to share your faith becomes an opportunity to avoid pushing someone even further away from Christ.*

These are situations of incredible victory for the Permission Evangelist. You can walk away with your head held high, knowing the joy of successful obedience to the Holy Spirit. You chose your soil carefully, and possibly coaxed a plot of land into asking for nourishment in the future. *Success in evangelism is obedience to the Holy Spirit, not saving souls.* God saves. We plant seeds where God tells us to—where he has prepared the soil. God won't leave fallow ground unplanted on purpose. The only time that happens is when someone isn't yet willing to answer the wooing call of the Holy Spirit.

If you can experience victory when you walk or when you talk, what constitutes failure in this process? Failure is disobedience to God's Spirit by attempting to do God's work without the Holy Spirit's guidance. If we engage in argument or conversation against the will of the Holy Spirit, we are acting out of our own pride—we sin—regardless of the intended outcome.

The Art of Debate—and How to Avoid It

"I have found the secret to eternal life" read the sign hanging across the shoulders of the man bearing striking resemblance to Woody Allen in a trench coat. Each week, with so many others, he filled his Sunday morning by wandering up and down the sidewalk past the "Christian Atheist," past the "King of the World," past tourists and the crowds that gathered in bewildered amusement at the heated arguments ensuing around each ladder. These simple stepladders are the modern day replacement for the wooden crate that gave birth to the phrase "on your soap box." The place is Speakers Corner in the northeast area of Hyde Park in London.

Set aside in 1872 for the specific purpose of allowing anyone to say anything he or she so desires (regardless of how contentious, ridiculous, or truly insane the message may be), this location has drawn many a famous person—from Karl Marx to Bob Dylan—to speak his mind amongst the trees. I first stumbled upon this spectacle in the early 1990s while in the United Kingdom for business and have since returned many times. It is truly a sight to behold as the throngs of sightseers, hecklers, Christians, Muslims, and some of the most unique people you will ever meet gather every Sunday from 7 A.M. to 7 P.M.

Immediately, as an American I was intrigued by the government-sponsored preservation of free speech, and the vigor with which so many exploited that right. As a Christian, I was surprised and encouraged by the number of religious discussions. A quick count revealed that over 90 percent of the speakers were espousing religious views, and even years before the disaster of September 11, 2001, the most heated discussions were between the Muslims and Christians. This was certainly not a microcosm of the world's beliefs, but an example of both the power of and failure of argument.

Many at Speaker's Corner are adept at making their point, turning the crowd against the "professional" hecklers, and keeping people engaged until they complete their oration. Some are good at drawing a crowd, such as the man that stood on his three-foot ladder adorned with a cowboy hat and Mardi Gras beads completely silent and unmoving for fifteen minutes just staring blankly into space. Remarkably, the largest crowd in the area formed around him before he uttered his first word. When he finally chose to speak he revealed his claim as the "King of the World" and began ranting almost incoherently about how we should be worshiping him, but I still stood there amused and listened, if only because I had waited so long.

Most of these sights were amusing, and a bit puzzling, but the longer I stayed, and every time I've returned, a sense of disturbing dread overcame me. The nutty guy advocating freedom of sex doesn't bother me, nor do the religious antagonists that disagree with my Christian point of view. What really disturbs me is the futility of public debate.

Certainly, most of these people speak with conviction because they believe what they say and believe that someone might possibly be changed by their words. I wonder, though, has anyone in modern times been changed by religious arguments delivered in this way? Although I know the famous stories of impactful change occurring in days gone by, I can think of no example in my life's experience.

I'm not saying others are not influenced by debate and argument. I can certainly recall the times when I was influenced by the arguments of others, but I was always influenced as an outside observer. The debaters are rarely changed, but the onlookers often are. And I find that the onlookers are impacted as much by the attitude and approach of those debating as they are swayed by the points of the argument.

For the same reasons Jesus never chased after anyone in an effort to convince them of his message, I am not at all opposed to backing out of a conversation if I realize the person's heart is not prepared to seek or accept truth. Sometimes it may be the wisest and most compassionate action. I may even need to take a temporary break from the relationship in order to keep future opportunities with that person open.

Some people argue without listening. If that's the case, no argument may make a difference. In those instances, it is appropriate to leave and present them with a clear step to take before you will re-engage. You leave the door open to future conversations with them, but they must be just as willing to make a fair effort.

A good example is a conversation with a devout antagonist that frequented my local coffee shop. This individual regularly ranted about organized religion to any Christian who would listen. He had previously been lured into a cult and carried many scars from that experience. On numerous occasions, I had seen him watching me studying my Bible and talking to friends, and we occasionally chatted. A pastor friend of mine had engaged him in conversation before our encounter and what resulted was a gush of hatred and distrust. My friend responded in a very intriguing way. When finally there was enough pause in the man's spewing to inject a thought, my friend simply said that he was sorry the guy had been so hurt, and he would pray for him to find peace in his life. A compassionate end to a conversation where no one was winning.

I liked that response, and for the situation, it seemed quite appropriate. My response was a little different when I had my encounter with the man because I had the benefit of my friend's encounter. When it was my turn to receive the vapid rant, I turned the tables. To his shock and horror, I asked, "Why are you saying these things to me? Are you attempting to convince me that your point of view is correct based on how it has so positively changed your life? Are you hoping that I will adopt the same opinion? Or are you asking me to challenge your statements because you would like to investigate if my point of view is correct and worth adopting? Those are two of the only three choices I can see. The third is you simply like to argue and need an audience. Which is it?"

He didn't respond. Expecting such a nonresponse, I quickly filled the dead air with a charge, "When you can answer that question with either of the first two answers, let me know and we'll continue this conversation as long as you would like. If, on the other hand, you just want to argue with no particular destination in sight, I'm not interested."

I bid him a good day, and excused myself. Sound harsh? Maybe, but when a person is unwilling to listen to reason, why on earth would you try to reason with him? If he was interested in seeking truth, or even enlightening me about his life-changing truth, I would have dug right in, but a pointless debate would simply leave both of us frustrated and angry. And what message would be communicated to the onlookers?

I could see in his face confusion at my confidence and unwillingness to try to convert him. He was challenging me to a duel, but it became obvious that I had no need to engage—not because I didn't care—but because I didn't need to win. *I was confident enough in my own beliefs to not require his belief as reassurance.* That's why he was confused, because he obviously needed that reassurance. Instead of arguing and creating discord, an opportunity was opened for a real conversation to occur when his heart was ready.

Summary
Numerous times, I have laid the groundwork for future conversations by leaving simple questions in someone's head. Getting permission to engage in a meaningful conversation about spiritual things that will lead to a discussion of Jesus begins with the creation of questions. As we have discussed throughout this chapter, leaving someone with questions is a great way to determine if he is being led by the Holy Spirit to seek answers and truth.

How do I know Permission Evangelism works? In the last few years, I have had hundreds of individuals ask me to tell my story. Let me stress this point: People *ask me* to tell my story. They ask me to tell them about Jesus. Is anyone asking you? They will ask you if you understand the process, listen to and obey the direction of the Holy Spirit, and honor each seeker's unique journey toward truth.

When truth-seekers engage with you and work their way through the process, they reach the point of asking you to tell them about grace. That grace is best described through your grace story—your personal account of your experience with God. This is the story they have asked to hear. If you think about it, as a Christian, every aspect of your life has a connection to God's grace. Discovering how to communicate that in a compelling way is the next step. There's power in your story. In fact, your story is about the greatest miracle that has ever occurred.

Prayer:

"Lord, teach me patience and give me the discernment to heed your Spirit's direction. Show me how to honor the spiritual journey of others, and never let my compassion for the lost wane. AMEN."

---

1. Seth Godin, Permission Marketing, Simon and Schuster, Copyright 1999, Page 136.

2. ibid, Page 46.

3. ibid, Page 80.

4. ibid, Page 96.

5. ibid, Page 142.

6. ibid, Page 47.

7. ibid, Page 131.

8. ibid, Page 137.

CHAPTER SIX

THE POWER OF STORY

1 Corinthians 1:22-29
Jews demand miraculous signs and Greeks look for wisdom, but we preach Christ crucified: a stumbling block to Jews and foolishness to Gentiles, but to those whom God has called, both Jews and Greeks, Christ the power of God and the wisdom of God. For the foolishness of God is wiser than man's wisdom, and the weakness of God is stronger than man's strength.
  Brothers, think of what you were when you were called. Not many of you were wise by human standards; not many were influential; not many were of noble birth. But God chose the foolish things of the world to shame the wise; God chose the weak things of the world to shame the strong. He chose the lowly things of this world and the despised things—and the things that are not—to nullify the things that are, so that no one may boast before him.

2 Corinthians 4:1-2,13
Therefore, since through God's mercy we have this ministry, we do not lose heart. Rather, we have renounced secret and shameful ways; we do not use deception, nor do we distort the word of God. On the contrary, by setting forth the truth plainly we commend ourselves to every man's conscience in the sight of God.

It is written: "I believed; therefore I have spoken." With that same spirit of faith we also believe and therefore speak …

Shy Scott's Story

At the end of the couch, Scott sat staring intently at the pillow nervously spinning between his fingers. Every word scraped across his lips with agonizing pain, and a normally articulate young man mumbled almost incoherently. Approximately twenty-five minutes had passed, and he was close to finishing the story of how he had come to know Christ almost twenty years earlier. He obviously detested this exercise.

At first, the reason seemed obvious, because Scott was shy. The idea of speaking about something very personal in front of a group of virtual strangers unnerved him. But after seeing this scene replayed over and over by other players, I realized that Scott's frustration was for a different reason. I had asked Scott, as well as the other nine attendees of the evangelism class, to tell me their conversion salvation story in the standard format—what their life before God was like, what their process of salvation was, and what the impact of God in their life had been since.

Because the people attending this course had accepted Christ at a young age, I expected this to be a simple task. But much to my surprise, I discovered that my questions exposed fears of inadequacy and a lack of confidence in the usefulness of their stories in sharing their faith.

Scott had stepped forward during an altar call when he was five years old. He knew exactly what he was doing and had never fallen away from God. His story was of a life kept free from the powerful effects of sin and rebellion. But like so many others who accept Christ in childhood, he struggled to see the value of his story to persuade the unbeliever.

It is no wonder that the Scotts of the world feel terribly inadequate in evangelism. They have seen the power of story and feel they don't have a story to tell! All of these people had heard the remarkable life-transforming stories of adult converts. They were simultaneously amazed by and disassociated from the stories of drug users, alcoholics, gang members, sex addicts and unscrupulous executives that turned to God and experienced sensational life transformations. It's the folks with the sensational life transformations or the famous professional athletes, rock stars, or politicians who are called upon to stand in front of the crowd and tell people about Jesus from the backdrop of their personal testimony. Why have we neglected the powerful testimony of those who have lived a life without rebellion and fear, hopelessness, and regret because of the sustaining presence of God in their lives from an early age?

One of the saddest things I have encountered in training Christians to share their faith is the child convert who believes that his or her grace story is less valuable in the evangelism process than that of the adult convert. Without considering their words, some have actually told me they wished they had not accepted Christ until later in life so they would have a more powerful story to tell to the unbeliever.

What an astounding lack of amazement about grace! I understand their pain, but to believe it is better to accept Christ later in life—to want to spend *less* time with God—grieves me. Why do we rejoice more at the adult convert who lived a life apart from God than for the person spared that pain? One, we are a sensationalistic society that feeds on the dramatic. We love excitement, stories of good versus evil, and heroes. Two, we never hear the story of the person that "didn't" because nobody ever asks. We have allowed our love of excitement and our hunger for the dramatic to affect our perspective of the story God is writing in every believer's life. God's plan for reaching the lost is never inadequate.

Our hunger for drama is oddly juxtaposed with our desire for realism. We demand inspiration through tangible, factual, historical events and claim to shun hype, but refuse to listen to the facts unless they entertain. We want our *Star Wars* science fiction, but require it to be *believable*. It is difficult for simply the facts of "imagined sins" and "potential pain," all avoided, to make for a believable or compelling story. We don't think that way, we don't tell stories that way, and we are not normally inspired that way. Facts are not enough. The life-long Christian needs to rediscover the wonder of God's enduring work of grace in his life.

Why the Wrong Emphasis

After hearing countless people share their faith, I've recognized that the typical structure for telling a personal story of salvation is skewed. About 80 percent of the story focuses on the "before" period—what life was like before accepting Christ as Savior. Another 15 percent of the emphasis is given to the process—how the individual came to Christ and the mechanics of asking Christ into your life. That leaves only 5 percent for grace—the transforming power of God in your life since becoming a Christian. This pattern also reflects many of the commonly taught methods of evangelism. What it most painfully ignores is that part of the story that is most appealing to the lost—grace and resulting hope for the future. After all, our call is not to always be prepared to give an answer for the sins of our past, is it?

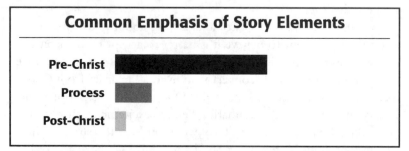

Common Emphasis of Story Elements

Pre-Christ	
Process	
Post-Christ	

Most Lives Are Not Lived in Extremes

I was teaching a ministry group led by a charismatic, well-spoken pastor considered by all to be a highly effective evangelist. When it came time for the attendees to share their personal stories, everyone begged him to go first, anticipating a dramatic conversion story that would inspire them to evangelize. Twenty minutes into his story, we had a great deal of facts about his 27 years without Christ. He laid out for us an incredible story with all the sins he had committed. The devastation of his life before Christ was deeper than most of us will ever know. He gave a fair amount of time to his process of conversion but had little to say concerning the impact on his life since, and nary a word about his future. Granted, he was speaking to Christians, and this was not a true evangelism moment, but the response of those listening was quite telling. The other Christians sat in awe, giving joyful witness to the miraculous transformation in his life. I could see them wishing their story showed such a dramatic change and wondering how they could be effective in evangelism.

They were missing a crucial point in an effective evangelism story—connection. The average person doesn't relate to such extremes. In fact, most unbelievers today would write off the dramatic conversion story to someone who had really hit rock bottom and had no where to go but up. They would view the salvation experience as a crutch, providing hope to someone who was hopeless. And while the unbelievers hearing such a story might be genuinely glad that person found something, anything, that helped, their happiness doesn't translate into personal conviction.

Most of today's non-Christians can't relate to such a story! They are living a "normal" life as determined by today's standards—where if someone is a positive, contributing member of society and isn't hurting anyone, including himself, he is on the right path and this *right path* does not necessarily require God, and even more rarely requires Jesus. It just requires that a person be on a journey to improve himself.

What is it in your story that will reach the masses seeking spiritual answers to life's questions? There is one aspect in every Christian's story that is sure to connect with anyone seeking truth, and it is all you need to tell. It is the story of grace. "Oh, that's easy," you may respond sarcastically, "and next you'll ask me to explain the Trinity!"

"Showing" Your Grace Story

Grace certainly is a tough subject and difficult to intellectually articulate—but not as difficult as you may think to communicate in a powerful way. Even if you've read some of the many books written about the topic of grace, and heard many a sermon, if you still struggle with putting it into words, you are in good company. That is precisely why it is best to not rely on just explaining grace intellectually, but rather, show it through your personal experience, just like the apostle Paul.

When I came to you, brothers, I did not come with eloquence or superior wisdom as I proclaimed to you the testimony about God. For I resolved to know nothing while I was with you except Jesus Christ and him crucified. I came to you in weakness and fear, and with much trembling. My message and my preaching were not with wise and persuasive words, but with a demonstration of the Spirit's power, so that your faith might not rest on men's wisdom, but on God's power. (1 Cor. 2:1-5)

Grace is more experiential than it is intellectual—a LOT more. Your experience with God is as individual as you are, and consequently, so is your understanding of grace in your life. In addition to being the core of salvation and quite an individual experience, it also has other unique characteristics that make it the perfect foundation for the evangelist's story. It doesn't require intelligence, education, evangelism training, proficiency in debate or being a great orator.

(1) Because you are communicating your personal grace experience, there is nothing to memorize or debate. *Explaining the hope that is in you requires only humility and obedience to the Holy Spirit's leading to change lives.*

(2) Because the grace in you is the reflection of God's Spirit, *your wisdom and eloquent speech are not necessary to make the message attractive to the lost.* God wants to *be* your wisdom and *be* your speech. Step away from the mirror, and let The Holy Spirit be reflected in you.

> Now the Lord is the Spirit, and where the Spirit of the Lord is, there is freedom. And we, who with unveiled faces all reflect the Lord's glory, are being transformed into his likeness with ever-increasing glory, which comes from the Lord, who is the Spirit. (2 Cor. 3:17-18)

(3) *Ignorance of grace is the one common denominator between every single person who does not have a personal relationship with Jesus Christ.* All unbelievers—Mormons, Hindus, Muslims, atheists, agnostics—lack the spiritual understanding of grace that only the Holy Spirit can provide. You may regularly run across an antagonist who can quote Bible chapter and verse better than you, or debate the latest scientific theory, but you will always have a leg up. You will *always* have something that you understand about God that they do not.

(4) Your experience of grace is true and irrefutable. Someone can argue the intellectual conclusion you came to, but he can't effectively argue your internal change nor the outward proof in the way your life is being lived. Your experience is true if you say so, and there is evidence of the presence of God in your life. The

positive results that have occurred because of your relationship with God force the unbeliever to consider that God exists. You are the living proof. All that remains is for you to learn to articulate your grace story in a way that emphasizes God's work of grace in your life.

What Is Your Story?

Before we can outline how to tell your story, let's first address why you tell your story at all. Most people think that the purpose of telling his or her story is to inform and educate the non-Christian about his or her need—the story of mankind's sin—the method for attaining salvation—Christ's perfect life, death, and resurrection. I agree all that needs to be communicated, but the purpose cannot solely be to educate unless he has agreed to take a test at the end of the conversation. There must be another objective or you will more often than not walk away feeling like a failure.

Think first of what God requires of the lost—to admit need, accept Christ's sacrifice, and ask for help. To get the unbeliever from where he is to where he needs to be requires knowing where he is in the first place because his salvation is based on his life—past and present—not yours. *The purpose for telling your story is simply to get him to tell you his. The seeker's story is the foundation of your salvation discussion and his ultimate decision.*

Mapping out Your Journey

Everything in your conversation should be leading to addressing two things: the seeker's need and Christ's ability to fulfill it.

To accomplish this, you must direct the conversation to the seeker's life, his pain, his understanding of a different way to live, and his steps to attain new life. Can you see how important THE SEEKER's story is? But since you must not interrogate him, how do you get him to peel back the layers and allow his story to unfold? You must use your story as a roadmap to guide him. Using your story, you walk him through several levels of trust until you have earned the right to challenge him to make a decision. The levels of trust that the non-Christian, eager for truth, walks through, include:

STEP 1: Your personal story might be intriguing enough to warrant the time to listen (you received permission).

STEP 2: You are safe to share information about their life situations or beliefs concerning God (you trusted them first).

STEP 3: Potential return is worth the investment of time for further investigation (reasonable anticipated benefit).

STEP 4: You are honorable enough to pose challenges to and consider their answers (you aren't trying to coerce or snow them).

STEP5: Answers merit decision (willingness to be challenged).

Think of your life like a roadmap of your country. What you really need to initially communicate is where your journey started, where it got off track, how you found your way to the right path, and what has happened since. A couple of major detours along the way are critical to know if you have had them, but what you want are single lines, not every mistake you ever made. You are selling the value of the destination, and they need to believe their path, although different, can lead to a similar, yet uniquely personal place.

Create a template with your story—one that the unbeliever can later follow in telling you his story—by mapping out your life in a very focused way:

You started in _____ (your childhood); traveled through _____ and _____ (your life experiences); received new directions that you listened to because _____ (how/why you began seeking truth); that new road was _____ (what was your process); and you found yourself _____ (what happened once you were saved). Use the worksheet in the back of the book (appendix C) to help you outline the elements of your story.

By focusing your story on certain key elements, you make it easier for them to lay their life out as a transparency over yours.

Compelling Emphasis of Story Elements

Pre-Christ	▎▎▎▎	*personal, revealing, brief*
Process	▄▄▄▄	
Post-Christ	█████████	*impact of God*

They may have started in a different place, and had different life experiences, but you will find a connection to their journey if you try. The critical point to remember in all this is not just the percentages of each segment of your story, but the *emotions* that were involved. The connection is made through the emotions you experienced along your journey.

Connecting with Feelings

The specific facts of your life and anyone else's will always be different. So communicating facts alone will not provide the connection you are seeking. When you attach an emotion to the pivotal moments in your story, you are demonstrating vulnerability and providing a powerful link to the person with whom you are sharing. For example, perhaps you grew up in poverty, neglected and abused, while the person you are in conversation with was living the wealthy high life. It would seem to be factually difficult to make a connection. But, if you talk about how you grew up feeling *alone and afraid,* even a rich kid (maybe *especially* a rich kid) might identify with those emotions. If the comfort from fear you discovered that allowed you to become a confident, peaceful adult was rooted in your relationship with Christ, they might decide it would be worth asking a few more questions if they could find help for their fear.

Choosing emotions isn't difficult, and you can't choose wrong. You can trust that God will bring people to you that will relate to your story. *When someone gives you permission to tell your story, believe that God has purpose in that interaction. Your obedience to his leading allows you to feel completely victorious regardless of the outcome.* You responded to questions about the hope that you have (1 Peter 3:15). If they give you permission to tell how God impacted your life, and you communicate the power of grace you experienced as emotional truths, they will be touched.

You can't choose the wrong emotions, because just about everybody has experienced the same ones. Boiled down, there are a few key emotions that almost everyone can relate to. When someone begins to recognize their understanding of a need for Christ, there are usually only a handful of emotions they connect to—such as loneliness, anger, grief—but in almost every single case, at the root you will find fear.

109

Don't worry, I'm not asking you to become a counselor, and that shouldn't be your purpose. Many people may never know *why* they act a certain way, and you don't need to understand the clinical issues, but you can communicate the biblical ones. What will lead them to engage and respond is truth.

As you express personal (biblical) truth, and use descriptive emotions in your delivery, people tend to respond in kind. Truth begets truth, and trust begets trust. It has been proven clinically that your true and pure expression of emotion will most likely stimulate some kind of inner emotional truth for the other person as well. It may be fear, anger, delight, or defensiveness. Whatever the response is, give thanks for that which is unfolding in them.[1]

Outlining Your Past

First step—write out everything that influenced your life direction and point of view about God. Did you go to church? Did you believe, but it never was real or personal enough to create change in your heart? Have you believed as long as you can remember? Were there sins against you, or sins that you committed, that impacted your life? Was there apathy, anger, or doubt? You get the gist.

Then when you read back through your pre-salvation specifics, look for patterns and emotions. After hearing the pastor's story I mentioned earlier, I asked, "In an emotion or two, sum up your childhood." He thought for a moment and said, "I guess throughout my entire childhood, I was alone and afraid." Twenty minutes of extremely unique experiences that few would connect to were summed up in a way that many can relate with.

I next asked him to tell me in a sentence, why. His response was that he had a very dysfunctional, uncaring family. Simple, personal, to the point, and something most people he will talk to about Jesus will relate to. There was an emotional impact he felt because of a life he didn't choose.

I asked him to do the same with his adult life—outline in a personally revealing way some of the lifestyle choices he had made. By this time he had figured out where I was going. He grouped his adult life into a couple of categories: seeking fulfillment through sex and success, and coming up emptier than before.

You need not reveal your darkest secrets, but you must open the door to show them that you are willing to be vulnerable. They must be confident that they are free to ask about your personal life. This may be the very first time that someone has trusted them. Trust breeds trust. If you reveal emotions and let them know there is information you are willing to give if they want to ask, they will often feel not only free to share their own story, but maybe even obligated.

If you accepted Christ as a child, in the process of discussing your childhood and adult life and decisions, outline the times when you doubted or stepped away from God, however brief. Connect emotions to those times of feeling alone, angry, or unforgiving. Then talk about how you came back to a deeper relationship with God just as the adult convert would talk about his conversion. What did you rediscover about God? What was affirmed so that you no longer doubt?

Outlining Your Conversion

When you outline your process of salvation, you must remember that you want the person to overlay his spiritual journey on top of yours. Otherwise, it will be difficult for him to draw parallels that leads him to ask more questions. To accomplish that, focus on two things:

1. Changes or discoveries in understanding/perspective (about God, Christians, Christ, life with God, etc.)

2. People and experiences that impacted those changes or discoveries.

It's pretty compelling when a seeker hears: "I once believed 'X,' but after getting to know this person and seeing his life with God, I began to ask questions. After a period of research and questioning, I saw that my original point of view was incomplete and I started seeking answers in the life of Christ. I wanted to know if it could be true." Do you know why this is so interesting to him? That is *exactly* where the person you are speaking with is at that moment in his life. He invited you to tell the story of your spiritual journey because he is seeking spiritual answers.

The seeker has doubts, or he would already believe. You are telling him that you had doubts too, and discovered that there are answers to be found *and you know how to do that.* How compelling. This also works if you've been in relationship with God since childhood. You can talk about a time when you walked away or doubted. Or, you can tell him about times of seeking for deeper meaning or clearer understanding. No matter when you accepted Christ as your Savior, you have been through times of testing— that's guaranteed in the Bible. So talk about those times and how you got through.

In addition, you are telling him about *people* that walked into your life, that you believe God led there, to introduce you to truth. Guess what, another "coincidence"—you just walked into *his* life. He will draw the parallel. To make sure, sometimes I even ask if he believes in coincidence, or if he thinks everything has a purpose. You'd be amazed at the percentage of people that believe the latter, bu don't think about it much. When presented with the possibility that his story might just be paralleling yours, without you even saying those words, he begins to listen more intently.

On numerous occasions I have been fortunate enough to witness the amazement of a non-Christian when he realizes that God has been alive in his life, wooing him. When he can look at the big picture and discover a series of experiences in a pattern created by God and not coincidence, he reaches a major milestone in the path to salvation. Time and time again, I have seen this moment of epiphany be the turning point that transitions argumentative resistance to Christianity to an honest pursuit of relationship.

Providing the Tools

An important aspect of outlining your decision process is to give the seeker all the tools he needs to accept Christ on his own. If you need to write out the picture of the chasm of sins with you on one side, God on the other, and Christ filling the gap (chapter 3), then do that. It's also good just to write down the steps of your decision in bullets on a napkin or piece of paper for him to take. Feel free to append verses to the points he might want or need to research on his own. At this point, you've already revealed what you believe, so it is easy to point to the Bible as the place to find more answers.

I suggest not giving a seeker a tract, though. As soon as you give him a pre-printed document, the personal, seemingly spontaneous interaction appears premeditated and manipulative. Feel free to get his e-mail or mailing address and follow up with a book or note, but always initially give him the steps to salvation verbally, in common language. Offering a follow-up is a great way to keep the conversation going and avoid a "hit-and-run" evangelism situation. In a world of instant, virtual communication, don't rely on face-to-face interaction only. Use every medium available to enable future conversations.

To be specific, when someone walks away after hearing your story, he needs to know enough to be able to act on his own whenever he is ready. A pastor friend of mine had his new neighbors over one night, and they asked him what he did for a living. He told them that a few years earlier he had left the life of an oil rigger to become a pastor. Curious, the wife asked how he got into "that." He told his story in a couple of minutes, gave the process he went through and outlined the subsequent change in his life. Her husband immediately changed the subject and it didn't come up again.

Unbeknownst to him, his next-door neighbor went home that very night and prayed to receive Christ. He only found out a month later when she asked for some marital advice. The resulting change in her had created tension in her marriage. The pastor hadn't deliberately laid out the steps of salvation for her but she knew all she needed to know because he was able to weave it conversationally into his personal story. This is critically important. After all, the end result you pray for is for them to accept Christ—but that doesn't mean it has to be done in your presence. You must prepare them just in case the two of you never speak again.

Although there are many ways to say it, here are the basic facts you should cover:

1. God created you for a relationship with him.
2. Your sins separated you from God.
3. God sent Christ to pay the penalty for your sins.
4. You believed and put your trust in Christ's death and resurrection.

The key is to weave these into your own story so they don't sound so clinical. Match up your own decision process with that of the Gospel. When did you believe God created you for a relationship? The story of your life without God should be prefaced with something like, "But I did a lot of stuff that separated me from God by selfishly making me the center of my life and not him." Then, when did your belief in Christ change, and how did that happen? Practice saying it aloud, and weave it into your story several different ways.

I have a lot of people tell me they believed when they were small children. If you are one of those people, you may or may not remember what you were thinking and feeling at that time. But I have no doubt that you can answer those questions from some other point in your life. Have you ever felt estranged from God because of your actions or attitudes? What did it take to bring you back into full fellowship with him? How did you feel before, during, and after? You get the picture.

The Punchline

Everything we have discussed so far should lead to the most important point—your life today and your future hope. Don't belabor the metamorphosis at the point of salvation—that's in the past. Talk about it as an ongoing, present miracle, not a one-time event. Instead of, "I stopped _____ that day and never did it again," try:

"I no longer live with that anger."

"I've learned that I can truly love other people without expecting anything in return."

"Since then I've been able to receive love and caring without feeling an obligation or feeling unworthy."

"Now I live my life with hope and an amazing peace. I know God is good and wants me to be peaceful. I know that although people will always fail, he'll absolutely never let me down."

As a Christian, the most important question you can ever answer for yourself is:

"What is the impact of God in my life today?"

If you're in the habit of living off of past successes, it may be difficult for you to answer that question. But it is vital that you do. Try it first only with emotions, and then attach the facts. If you can't answer what the positive impact of God in your life has been, you will never be able to effectively reach the lost. If you believe God has done no miracle in your life, you must address your personal relationship first.

114

This isn't about merely a life-change (e.g., I'm no longer an alcoholic), this is about expressing a heart change. List a couple of those specific lifestyle changes, but more importantly: Do you see people differently now? Do you see yourself differently? Do you see God differently? Do you love or receive love differently? What bad emotions were replaced with positive emotions?

And what is ongoing? What do you believe about your future? What are you confident about? How is your peace manifested? What is your hope based on? How are you living the rest of your life differently because of your very intimate and personal relationship with God?

Everything else you tell a non-Christian is interesting and may connect them with your journey, but until they believe that their heart change can resemble yours, everything else is insufficient. God didn't make it so alcoholics can only reach alcoholics. Your life and your story does not need to exactly mirror theirs. The only thing that they need to connect with is a desire for truth, a journey that involved questions and answers and a positive impact from the result you found. Too many specific details of your life can get in the way. If they can't see the big picture of your salvation and draw a personal parallel, it becomes more about you than them. They can simply walk away and say, "I'm glad *you* found God and that helped *you*."

If you ever hear a statement similar to that, be assured they heard facts and not God's Spirit. Ask yourself if you really gave of yourself, or just told a tale. Did you give something up? Did you risk anything? Facts don't draw people to God, the Holy Spirit does. Get out of the way.

> Therefore, since we have such a hope, we are very bold. We are not like Moses, who would put a veil over his face to keep the Israelites from gazing at it while the radiance was fading away. (2 Cor. 3:12-13)

When you tell someone about the impact of God in your life, are you *naturally* smiling? If not, I don't think you really have grasped the magnitude of what has occurred in your life. Are you overwhelmed by the fact that the Creator of the universe chose to be in an intimate relationship with *you*? Man, I am. Brand new

Christians are. You should be too. Don't let your joy fade into a distant memory. After all, the angels are still dancing.

It's a Wonderful Life, Isn't It?

If you are finding the answer to that question difficult, here's some homework. Imagine your life without God. Go back as many years as you can and look at all the times you could have died, been hurt, or could have walked away. Pretend much of that happened, and play out a story in your head of what would have become of you. If you think your life would have ever been better if you weren't a Christian, we've just stumbled upon the reason why you fail in evangelism—you don't believe. You must address this now and it may take a while. Express your doubts to your pastor or someone else you can trust. Pray for God to make himself real, and pray for the desire to know him. This is a good place to be, because it will lead you to draw closer to God than ever before. But you must push through, ask all the questions, and don't give up on searching for answers.

Think this never happens? Believe me, it does. In the middle of teaching an evangelism workshop, I have had individuals recognize and confess their need, often shocking everyone else in the room. Sometimes, the "good and faithful, lifelong Christian" has been living his or her parent's faith, or have been a social Christian. Sure, they have had questions from time to time, but there are few safe places in church for a Christian to ask questions about their own salvation without fear of rejection.

Ask the questions. Please, express your doubts. If your church and friends don't accept you afterward and embrace you with broken hearts, get a new church and new friends. This is about being true to God and to you. Don't put on the happy face—*be* happy! Don't feign peace—*be* peaceful! Seek God. If you haven't found him in a life-changing personal way, surround yourself with people who will help in that process.

Wrapping It All Up

Now that you have the three major components of your story, wrap it all up together. I hesitate to put time limits on it, because then you risk practicing too much and deliver it the same every time.

If so, eventually, it will sound staged and pre-rehearsed. Instead, practice it a few times and just try to keep it reasonably brief.

You should seek to flow with the conversation and look for body language to let you know if you should continue or back off. If someone is looking away, laughing or snickering, or fidgeting a great deal, stop and address his reaction. If he doesn't want to hear your story, don't continue. If he just looks uncomfortable, attempt to ease his tension.

Sometimes, before I tell my story, I say something to let them know that I may be just as nervous telling it as he may be listening. Often, after someone asks me to tell how I came to believe in God or have this relationship with Jesus (really, they do); I say, "Well, this is kinda personal, but I'm happy to tell you if you want to know." Half the time he'll be almost a little embarrassed and say, "I'd like to know, but don't feel obligated or pressured."

Of course, I always relent. Think about it. People regularly apologize for asking me to tell them about Jesus! How cool is that? I'm not deceiving them because my story really is personal. I don't just give them facts; I tell them the real deal and let them know they can ask me anything. I draw them into my life so that they will draw me into theirs. I'm vulnerable so they will feel safe responding in kind. If they don't today, they will eventually.

When you deliver your story in a personal, vulnerable, and believable way, no self-respecting person who asked to hear it would argue the specifics. If the person does become argumentative or attack, you need to work on the permission process and discerning where the Holy Spirit is leading. If this happens repeatedly, you are likely operating under your own power and not allowing God to guide the right people to you.

Call to Action

After delivering your story, they will either ask questions to get more details, tell you their story, or redirect the conversation. If they ask questions to garner more details about some aspect of your story, they are revealing the connection to their story that you have yet to hear. That's exactly why an outline of several points concerning your past is best rather than depth concerning a single point. Give them several opportunities for connection.

In my own story, although my relationship with God is always changing, and he still has much work to do with me, the points I usually address are:

Pre-Christian Childhood
- religious history (no solid structure—tried a lot of faiths)
- family issues (divorce and moved a lot)
- personal struggles (loneliness and sense of abandonment)

Pre-Christian adult
- became anti-Christian and very angry
- tried to fill emptiness with sex and success
- always came up emotionally empty

Process
- Christian entered my life and challenged me
- I began a quest to prove Christianity false
- Did a lot of research, and became a Christian ten months later

Postconversion
- I've discovered that being a Christian makes me strong, not weak
- I have a new definition of success, and am blessed beyond my wildest imagination
- I have learned to love unconditionally and openly receive love
- I have forgiven my parents and mended those relationships
- I have purpose and meaning in my life and know where I am going
- I have incredible peace and hope concerning my future

I hesitate to write it out as a single story because I rarely tell it in one breath without some discussion, but I'm forced to leave that up to your imagination. I watch their body language. Something always tips a particular interest. As I tell my story I seek points of connection with their life. Any sign that tells me they relate is where I choose to expand. I'll abandon much of my story as soon as I find that connection and encourage them to open up a little. With that in mind, as you read this, picture the many places that I could pull them into the conversation.

An example of how I would tell my story:

I attended a lot of churches as a child, but was really put off by what I saw as hypocrisy and blind faith, so I rejected Christianity because of my perspective of Christians. My parents were divorced when I was young, and I lived a very lonely childhood. I didn't get much direction or attention as a kid and became fiercely independent and resentful. When I was young I was a shy bookworm that desperately desired to be accepted, so as I entered my teen years I went to extremes to fit in, doing many things I now regret.

As an adult, I sought power and accomplishment as a means to fill the emptiness in my life. I thought if I got the next beautiful woman, or ran the company, I would be able to rest and find peace, but nothing ever satisfied. There was a time, one night, lying in bed with a woman I hardly knew, that I hit bottom. It was my sister's wedding earlier that day, and it dawned on me that my sister loved someone so much that she was willing to commit her life to be with him. But my heart was so black and empty that I didn't care if anyone I knew lived or died. I realized that I would never be able to experience the joy my sister knew that day because I was incapable of love. I couldn't receive it or give it. That night I cried for the first time in years. I felt as though my life was hopeless, and I was doomed to loneliness.

Soon, thereafter, a woman came into my life that challenged my point of view. She was intelligent, successful, beautiful, and surprisingly, a Christian. When challenged, she had answers and then challenged me. I realized that I didn't really have a belief system that I could clearly articulate. I was anti-Christian, but not pro-anything else. I called myself an atheist, but held out for a God "just in case."

The next day I set out to prove Christianity false, starting with the New Testament accounts, in an attempt to awaken her to "logic and truth." I studied science, philosophy, Christian and non-Christian points of view. I discovered that the existence of God actually proved many scientific theories because those theories contradicted basic facts without a creator. I learned that God created me to have a relationship with him, but I did things in my life to prevent that relationship. I started attending a church that addressed my mind as well as my heart, and that's where I learned about Jesus dying for my sins so that

I could reconnect with God forever. It was hard to understand until I saw the impact on those that believed.

I began to get to know people whose lives weren't necessarily better than mine; in fact, many were technically worse, but there was something about them. They were genuinely happy. They had hope and peace that you could see on their faces. They had bad stuff going on in their lives, but responded differently than I would. Some time after that I stopped trying to prove Christianity false, and started wondering if it was true.

Once I began to seek truth, answers came. One night, ten months after my quest had begun, I decided that it took more faith to believe in anything else. I made an intellectual decision to believe Christ died for my sins and that if I accepted his gift and turned my life over to God, my heart would change. I prayed, and the most incredible thing happened. After I made that intellectual decision, I experienced a spiritual and emotional result that was miraculous. It really defies description, but I felt the weight of the world lift off my shoulders. For the first time in my life, I felt forgiven, clean, and loved. I cried again that night, but this time, it was out of joy.

From that moment forward my life has changed. My anger began to dissipate; not immediately, but through the years, I have become able to forgive and love. I have learned to give of myself without expectation for something in return, and I'm always amazed at how it changes me. I am now not only capable of giving love, but I can accept it without feeling obligated or guilty.

I thought I would have to give up my drive for success when I became a Christian, but God made me successful anyway. He just showed me how to do it without hurting others in the process. I now seek answers and direction from God when life doesn't make sense, and I know where to go. I've had so many miracles in my life since I developed a personal relationship with God that I will never doubt again. I have so much peace and hope that I expect incredible things to happen all the time.

God used people to impact my life and teach me how to discover truth. It was not a chance happening when those people came into my life. The timing was too perfect. It could be that you are experiencing something similar. It just might not be chance that I happen to have entered your life at this exact time.
Silence.

The Seeker's Turn

Let it linger. Don't give in to the uncomfortable, pregnant pause in conversation. Make the seeker say the next word. He will reveal where the conversation should go. If he asks a question about what you've said, that is your point of connection. Ask yourself why he chose that question. If someone asks me, "What books did you read?" or "How did you find that church?" I can offer him a book or invite him to church.

If he asks a specific question about your past, he is likely experiencing the same issue or emotion. Reveal more specifics, but all the while try to make him comfortable with revealing some truth to you. What you'll likely find is people saying, "I don't know why I'm telling you this, but ..."

It happens a lot when you are vulnerable. People feel safe and spill their guts.

If he changes the subject, don't fight it. Don't press the issue. You just created a great deal of questions in his head. You didn't give him all the answers. One or two things you said will stay with him, and that's what you should pray for. He will be plagued with the desire to know more and may eventually approach you. He may just blurt out a question months later, or you might just find that you simply run into him more.

If so, God is directing him to continue the conversation. Let him bring it up again, unless you clearly see that he wants to talk but are uncomfortable. Many, many times, I've said to someone, "Last time we talked, I know it got kinda heavy. Did anything I say make you uncomfortable? Do you have any questions about it?" Even if he says no, let him know that if he ever does, you are more than happy to talk about it, and then drop it.

That tells him that you won't bring it up again, and he can feel comfortable hanging out with you, unafraid that you will drag him into a heavy discussion about God. You must put the ball in his court, but let him know you are prepared and willing to play. The door must stay cracked open and inviting, not ominous and scary. He knows the facts and the possibilities. He has no reason not to trust you, and he has heard the Gospel and what is required of him.

If you struggle with leaving the ball in his court and prayerfully waiting, remember that Jesus got it! Jesus didn't chase the young ruler (Luke 18:18-27). The next step is God's and theirs. Trust in God and rejoice for the opportunity to play a part in their salvation. Pray for their desire for truth to overwhelm their pride, and await an opening or invitation to re-engage. In the meantime, just love them and serve them. Don't expect anything from them, and they will fall in love with God's Spirit in you.

---

1 http://sourcecounseling.com/List.html.

CHAPTER SEVEN

BEING IN THE WORLD

In the long run, we get no more than we have been willing to risk giving.

—Sheldon Kopp[1]

Sometimes we are to guard our heart...protect it from invasion and keep things safe and secure. Sometimes we should give our heart...let certain qualities out and release them to others.

—Charles Swindoll[2]

Mark 2:13-17

Once again Jesus went out beside the lake. A large crowd came to him, and he began to teach them. As he walked along, he saw Levi son of Alphaeus sitting at the tax collector's booth. "Follow me," Jesus told him, and Levi got up and followed him.

While Jesus was having dinner at Levi's house, many tax collectors and "sinners" were eating with him and his disciples, for there were many who followed him. When the teachers of the law who were Pharisees saw him eating with the "sinners" and tax collectors, they asked his disciples: "Why does he eat with tax collectors and 'sinners'?"

On hearing this, Jesus said to them, "It is not the healthy who need a doctor, but the sick. I have not come to call the righteous, but sinners."

For the Love of Sinners

Levi, the dishonest tax collector, came face to face with Jesus and was changed forever. He must have known that Jesus was anointed by God and certainly had heard of his miracles and teaching because Christ was in his city for some time. Accustom to the hatred and shunning by the religious leaders of Capernaum, I wonder if Levi cringed when he saw Jesus coming his way? I'm reasonably certain he wasn't expecting Jesus, the miracle worker, to honor him with a personal invitation. After Levi decided to follow Jesus, he didn't suddenly have a whole list of new, "more acceptable" friends. In fact, he opened his home to those he knew needed an introduction to Jesus, welcoming people of all walks of life to share in his joy.

Imagine it! The nosy, self-righteous religious leaders slinking up to see what all the commotion is about—hoping to "get the goods" on Jesus, but refusing to step into Levi's house because of the reputations and lifestyles of those in attendance. What a pitiful sight—their self-righteous attitude kept them from a personal encounter with God. Their pride prevented them from experiencing the joy of seeing others meet God. How more gracious and accepting is the man who has a right picture of himself, than the self-righteous man.

The leaders saw the sinners only by their deeds because they judged themselves by the same criteria. God sees our works, but his gaze lingers on our hearts. More than our actions, our hearts reflect our desire to know and be known by God. The scribes and Pharisees only saw the visible half of humanity, the shallow veneer that glossed over and protected the reality of the person inside. Their failure was not the assessment of the sinners, which was fairly accurate, but rather their overestimated assessment of themselves.

The Allure of Personal Repentance

I attended a remarkable church in Utah that went through some tough times. Mostly, it was a church of community, relationship, and love where all were accepted. Any given Sunday there would be young doctors, homeless people, lawyers, unwed mothers, students, executives, drug addicts, simple laborers—anyone desiring truth and needing acceptance where they were in their journey. It was not what one would call a traditional "seeker sensitive" church, but I would call it "seeker attractive" nonetheless. We passed Bibles out in every service, never shied away from visual symbols of faith, and addressed every message with the fervent conviction that biblical truth was the key to the answers of life. Of course, the guy that tossed the Bibles down the aisle was barefoot and had dreadlocks past his waist, one of the pastors was a guitar-playing ski bum, and the other was a former competitive body builder and self-professed Jesus freak.

Still the church quickly grew to about 125 in a culture more resistant than most in the U.S. toward Christianity—Mormon-entrenched Utah. Many of the local, traditional, established churches kept a watchful eye on this rapidly expanding band of misfits, expecting us to fall apart any day. Their predictions appeared to be at hand when our lead pastor fell into sin and committed adultery. He repented immediately, confessed to his wife at their first meeting, and then called all of the leaders of the church together (about twenty of us) to confess, ask our for-giveness, and resign. He was leaving town to attempt to repair his relationship with his wife and hopefully salvage his marriage.

I had the impression that he never really expected us to forgive him. He was obviously afraid to ask. He could hardly look into our eyes as the weight of his shame seemed to visibly crush his body. It was the most touching, tearful evening of my life. We saw true repentance from a thoroughly broken man, and God touched our hearts. We prayed, we cried, and many hours after he had left, we all went home.

That evening as we all lay awake in disbelief, the possible rami-fications filled our thoughts. There were questions too numerous to contemplate, but eventually our concerns turned to the church and its future. What would become of those who trusted our leader, especially the new Christians and those still investigating? They came to our church because it was the only place they had discovered in that city where they felt challenged, yet accepted. Would they all leave? Should we be prepared to see our once bustling church drop 50 percent or more? How would the reputa-tion of the church impact the hundreds of thousands still lost in our city? How could God possibly use this?

Our assistant pastor, Jeffrey, a very intense man filled with the love of God and passionate about reaching the lost, was away at a retreat during this tumultuous time. We had no way to reach him.

When he returned two days after our pastor resigned, he responded in a way none of us expected. He encouraged us all to continue the prayer groups we had started on our own after the event. In fact, he challenged us to intensify our prayers, but he changed our focus from the problem at hand to our own sin. He guided us toward introspection and called us to get right with God as individuals. He also encouraged us to repent of our participation in the sin of our pastor.

Our participation? For the first time, we wondered if we over-looked the signs. Had we been reaching out, asking the questions, making him accountable? Had we missed opportunities to embrace the woman involved and help fill the voids in her life that caused her to seek solace in sex? Were we lusting in our own hearts? Were we simply one bad decision away from being just like them?

Jeffrey called us to analyze our past, present, and expectations for the future. Were we judging either of them? Was anger ruling our thoughts and actions? Did we doubt God could use this for his glory? Were we afraid of our own reputations? Through prayer and the leading of the Holy Spirit, the answers came, and for many, me included, we were quite convicted.

He forced us to acknowledge the sin our leader and our friend committed and not shy away from the reality of its impact. We learned to look more critically at our own lives, deeds, and most of all, our hearts. In short order, we were no longer focused on the future of the church because our own need for repentance and God's Spirit in our lives consumed our prayers. I have never seen humility of that magnitude before or since sweep through a body of believers. Jeffrey preached, everyone prayed, and the city gossiped. Three months later, we looked up from our prayers and our small band of 125 or so weekly visitors had more than doubled to over 300.

It wasn't the preaching that changed; although a powerful speaker, Jeffrey had spoken at that church since the beginning. It could not have been our production, because that suffered greatly during those months. The only thing that changed was our hearts. We prayed more, we loved each other more, and our unworthiness for salvation stared us square in the face every waking hour. It made us amazed at the impact of God in our lives and the freedom by which we could only live with him as our guide. We forgave our pastor, our friend who sinned with him, we forgave each other, and we forgave ourselves.

People came forward and confessed their own sins, either in small groups or in front of the whole congregation. We kept a vision of our own hearts in all their filth and beauty as time and again we were called to personal repentance and forgiveness of others. We lived a vibrant, active, and public life of acceptance, repentance and forgiveness. When we blew the dust of self righteousness off our hearts, the Holy Spirit shone like a beacon guiding anyone in need of spiritual repair to the safe passage found in that place.

Unlike the religious leaders that judged Levi and his compatriots, we were able to see the sins of the sinful and look honestly at the sin in ourselves. Because of our equal knowledge of Christ and how he honors us with acceptance and salvation, our hearts and heads did not droop long. Visitors to that church were drawn to our simultaneous humanity and holiness. Our joy in humility was more attractive than any service we ever produced.

Most of the people involved in that miracle, including myself, no longer live in that city or attend that church, but I often pray that I can continue to experience personal and corporate humility before God. There can be nothing more attractive to the sinner, and more repelling to the prideful. Christ embraced, honored, and dined with sinners because he had God's heart. As individuals, and as the church, we are called to develop that very same heart.

Reputation Matters

Contrary to popular belief, I believe Christ was very concerned about his reputation.

Christ even took steps to set the record straight on his character and intentions by healing the ear of the servant of the High Priest in the Garden of Gethsemane (Luke 22:51). He removed the evidence of the resistance of his disciple to set the record straight on his intention. He didn't want anyone to claim that his crucifixion was anything other than voluntary. Don't tell me Christ was not interested in his own reputation. He wanted to make sure everyone knew the facts of who he was and what he claimed. He died because the reality of God's love as he expressed through word and deed contradicted their idea of righteousness. The leaders, blinded by their pride, were already dead. They killed Christ because they feared his reputation.

Christ didn't just hang out with sinners; he initiated contact, enjoyed their presence, accepted their gifts, and publicly defended them. He let them know that he sympathized with the plight of the impact from their sins, but never condoned those sins, participated in them, or hid his concern. Christ went to great lengths to let the lost know he understood them, honored them, and had their best interests in mind even to the point of death.

They all knew where he stood on sin. He told them. But, his actions clearly demonstrated that he loved them, and those people, the only ones whose opinions really mattered, understood his reputation perfectly. I don't believe telling them about love would have been sufficient, just as telling the sinners in our church that we loved them would not have impacted their lives without us showing that love. We never condoned their sin, but we ate with them, prayed with them, cared for them, and called them to repentance.

Christ went to where the broken, sick, and sinful people could be found. He did not demand their repentance before he spent time with them. For many, like Levi, the fact that Jesus would spend time with them was the necessary step for their salvation. Things are not so different today. Many Christians have so removed themselves from "the world" that not only are they safe from the world's influence but the world is safe from any influence Christ might have through them. What a pity! It's not what Jesus would do.

Where Do You Fish?

How now shall we live? Christ, born holy, spent time with sinners; but even the majority of adult converts have no non-Christian friends—none—within two years of conversion. And those who have grown up in the church? There is no number less than none. I spoke at a workshop in North Carolina and mentioned that I took yoga classes. I was stopped cold by a woman in the second row. She had expressed the desire to do the same thing but didn't because of the concerns of her Christian friends. She asked with wide eyes how I could do something like that since a lot of yoga teachers practice Buddhism and chant in class.

I simply said, "Because there are no Christians there; because some teachers practice Buddhism and chant in class; and because although I am not tempted to believe what they say or act upon it, others in the class are." Just a few days earlier, a friend remarked, rather surprisingly, that he noticed that I spent more time with non-Christians than Christians. "Of course," I said. "If there were more Christians doing these activities, I wouldn't be alone!"

I told both of them that when I lived in Utah I developed a heart for the people resistant to all religion because of the oppressive Mormon influence. I wanted to reach those people, and I knew where to find them. Sunday mornings when the Christians and Mormons were in church, those people were in the parks, the coffee shops, and the restaurants. I would occasionally skip church and go to the park to hang out with the kids in the drum circles.

They had built a community of acceptance by being unacceptable together. Many did drugs and drank excessively. Others practiced tarot card reading and all manner of dark arts. My friends would dance with them, play drums in the public circles or jump into a game of Hacky Sack. Sometimes we shared a drink or sandwich or tossed a Frisbee. We prayed for them and occasionally were able to talk about Christ. At the very least, we understood them better and our compassion for the lost grew.

How many non-Christians do you spend time with? Are you so tied up in Christian activity that you don't have time for anyone but Christians? Do you expect non-Christians to reach out to you first and conform to your ideals without the grace of God?

I acted in a short drama at a church in Atlanta on this exact subject. The message struck a convicting chord throughout the congregation. I played a seeker who had been invited to church by a Christian co-worker. Struck by the message, questions abounded, and my character was eager to pursue answers with his friend. Seeking a time to arrange a meeting, the Christian consulted his pocket calendar. Monday: prayer meeting; Tuesday: Bible study; Wed: church; Thursday: church planning meeting; Friday: dinner with pastor; Saturday: evangelism training course; Sunday: church (of course); the entire next week: youth retreat. The Christian friend offered to call him in a couple of weeks and set something up, thanked him for coming, and ran off to attend a church committee meeting.

Standing solemnly, alone in a solitary pool of light, I stared out at the audience. Dropping my head, I slowly began to walk away; then I stopped, turned to address the audience, and said, "Anybody wanna go to lunch?"

Blackout.

You could have heard a pin drop. Although it was customary to clap after dramas in my church, nobody moved. Silence. My acting skills leave a great deal to be desired, so I know it wasn't the delivery; it was the message. That story spoke truth, and God used it. Although the situation was extreme to make the point with humor, not many people laughed that Sunday. They were forced to look at their own lives and assess whom they were trying to please, reach, and love. Was their zeal for serving their church getting in the way of serving God by loving their non-believing neighbor? Harsh question, I know, but worth asking.

I know several of my friends did an assessment of their own calendars, reset some priorities, and a few future church events were a little less attended. I think our pastor was glad. My friends rightfully sought balance between their church activities and being in the world, rubbing shoulders with the unchurched. My friends and my pastor knew that the greatest good you can do for the church is the good you do outside the walls.

Boundaries in Evangelism

While I do encourage you to step out of your comfort zone and get involved in activities and events outside the church, you still need the church and the church needs you. Nobody is immune to temptation, and we all must respect the steps that lead us to sin. Satan likes nothing better than to lure you into sin through acts of evangelism. In the back of my Bible, I have written:

"You know the blows you are dealing Satan,
  by the blows that are returned."

If you are involved in the heat of battle for souls, expect opposition. Expect it to sneak up on you; expect it to scare you from the work of God and drive you to the safety of the ever-inviting

Christian "holy huddle." I know a pastor that experiences migraines every Monday, with pain equal to the movement of the Spirit in the service the day before. I know ministers regularly tortured by temptations and Christians lured into sin because they just wanted to be accepted by their non-Christian friends so that they could witness to them. I have seen good men fall in the midst of righteous intentions and godly enthusiasm because they practiced ignorant boldness.

Evangelism can be scary even when you are in a safe environment like your home or workplace, so how do you protect yourself when you step out of the safe zone and into the real world? The first key is to understand your limitations. You must know what your *sin steps* are.

> So, if you think you are standing firm, be careful that you don't fall! No temptation has seized you except what is common to man. And God is faithful; he will not let you be tempted beyond what you can bear. But when you are tempted, he will also provide a way out so that you can stand up under it. (1 Cor. 10:12-13)

As Christians, we spend too much time worrying about avoiding sin. It isn't the sin that we should focus on avoiding. It's not like you're sitting at home, minding your own business, and "poof" you're in adultery, or "all of a sudden" you're smoking crack. For some people, those sins are not their issues, and they could walk right into a crack house and talk to an addict or pray with hookers in the red light district in Amsterdam without temptation taking hold. For others, just driving within sight of a particular neighborhood alone is sinful.

> When tempted, no one should say, "God is tempting me." For God cannot be tempted by evil, nor does he tempt anyone; but each one is tempted when, by his own evil desire, he is dragged away and enticed. Then, after desire has conceived, it gives birth to sin; and sin, when it is full-grown, gives birth to death. (James 1:13-15)

Sin steps are the little, seemingly, inconsequential decisions we make that lay the groundwork for volitional acts of sin. You may think that your sins—even your big ones—are involuntary, but they aren't. You may not desire to sin or willingly decide to take that final step, but you do choose to put yourself at risk with those small steps of little decisions. They build upon each other and pave a clear path to those things we swear we will never do again. Those baby steps of conscious decision must be avoided, or sin will always sneak up on you. Identify them, avoid them, and consider them sin. Seek freedom in knowing that God would never put you at risk. If you feel burdened for someone in a place that would be a compromise for you, trust there are other ways for that person to be led into a relationship with God. God desires you to remain pure, and he desires the lost to be found, but he will never compromise one for the other.

Reckless Love Wrecks Lives

Anton was one of my top employees. He had only worked for the computer networking company I managed for a few months, but it was obvious to all that he was very bright. He always had a smile on his face, was helpful and cordial to everyone, and I quickly grew to trust him. One Tuesday, bright and early, Anton left with one of our company cars to start his daily rounds of service calls and drop off some computer equipment that had been repaired. Everything in the morning ran according to plan, and then about 3:00 in the afternoon one of my employees walked into my office with concern on her face.

Anton had made all of his morning calls without incident, finished his 11:00 A.M. appointment early, but never showed up for his 1:00 P.M. service call. We contacted his other afternoon appointments just in case he had gotten his schedule confused, but he was nowhere to be found. We knew that if he was in an accident the police would call the office because he was in a company car, so there was no point calling hospitals. We were left to wait anxiously. After 6:00 P.M. passed with no news, I called his wife, but she had heard nothing. I stayed at the office until 10:00 P.M. that night, but Anton seemed to have disappeared off the face of the earth.

The next morning there was still no sign. Anton's wife still had not heard anything, and we became extremely concerned. It was about twenty-four hours later when Anton's wife contacted the office to say he would be calling me later that day. What I heard was shocking.

Anton was a Christian and studying to be an ordained minister. He was a deacon at his church and carried his Bible everywhere he went. At the time, I was nowhere close to being a Christian, so none of that had a positive influence on me. Even though he was a rather zealous Christian, I still respected him, which was not common for me at the time. But the rest of his story made me consider Christians more delusional than I originally thought.

Anton was a crack addict. He had accepted Christ and been clean for quite some time. He even was part of a ministry designed to reach out to addicts and dealers in the low-income neighborhoods of inner-city Atlanta. He often teamed up with another member of the ministry and boldly traveled right into the heart of the same drug havens he frequented as an addict, praying with dealers and challenging other addicts to seek a better life through faith in God. His testimony and boldness were impressive. His resolve to help troubled youth touched even me, the atheist, but his ignorance had me shaking my head.

The day Anton disappeared he had a business appointment within a few miles of one of the neighborhoods he regularly frequented with his ministry. Because he had finished his last morning call early, he found he had two free hours. It was too far to drive back to the office, so he skipped his lunch and traveled into that seedy neighborhood with hopes of helping a lost soul. Although he was alone, he was confident in his salvation and subsequent freedom from drugs. He was certain he could withstand temptation because he had done it so many times before without incident. I knew that a non-Christian recovering addict would not have been so confident, and never would have entered that den of temptation alone, but Anton thought that his faith saved him from the pull of sin.

Anton was dead wrong. Without the accountability, prayers and wisdom of his ministry partner, Anton quickly found himself face to face with his past, armed with a tin foil bullet and a sidearm crack pipe. He recounted how, just a short time later, the crack was gone, as well as any cash he had on hand. Within four hours, he was walking out of a pawnshop with pennies on the dollar for the customer's computer equipment he was scheduled to deliver hours earlier.

He said that he vaguely remembered where he left the car, but was willing to go search for it on the way to rescue the computer equipment from pawn. Later that day he arrived at the office, equipment and car keys in hand, and sat down in my office while his wife waited in the parking lot, too embarrassed to come in. I won't recount the entire conversation for you, but I gave Anton another chance. He returned to work under the condition he would never miss a Narcotics Anonymous meeting, never stray from his appointment schedule, and would check in several times a day. He performed fine for a little while, but soon stumbled once again, and I had to let him go. His initial fall had enabled drugs to reestablish a foothold that was very difficult to unseat, leading to his second drug binge. Before he would be back to normal, he would have to submit to extended counseling to free himself and return to the road of a successful recovering drug addict.

I saw Anton again years later at a computer trade show and he looked well. He was advancing in his career and had become a fully ordained minister. His marriage was strong, and it was obvious he was joyful and grateful to be alive. Anton had learned the powerful pull of sin, and most importantly, the small steps that weakened his resolve to turn from it.

Anton's failure wasn't evangelism, or even choosing to reach those still lost in the very place God had pulled him from. God will often choose to use the pain of your past to connect with another's present. That isn't always something to be avoided, as your personal testimony and evidence of the freedom from sin is the best demonstration of the power of God. Those stories give hope to the hopeless, and if you've been in the same place, you have earned the right to speak frankly without reservation.

Anton knew this, and his intentions were honorable, but his failure was in underestimating the steps that led to his sin and not protecting himself from them. I believe he still ministers in those neighborhoods, but he no longer goes alone. He surrounds himself with prayer, accountability, and other people. Anton is still trusting God, but not himself.

Anton's compassion overshadowed his logic, making him vulnerable. His honorable intentions, left unprotected by the presence of another believer and prayer, exposed him like a warrior wielding a sword on the battlefield with nothing but his underwear on. I know it's an odd analogy, but my point is that often it is the simple, common things that keep the warrior from focusing on the battle at hand. When you are engaged in the war for souls, you dare not go on the battlefield unprotected and distracted by influences whose power is magnified in your weakness.

Balancing Judgment, Compassion, and Protection

Being the most effective evangelist you can possibly be requires not only understanding the non-Christian but also understanding yourself. Taking risks is part of evangelism, and I encourage you to step out in faith as often as you can. Step out into the world, but be wary of a world that wants nothing more than for you to fall flat on your face. Trusting God does not mean being reckless with temptation.

A Christian friend of mine, a natural evangelist who lived a life of excessive sex and drugs before accepting Christ, shared with me an exciting story of how he was able to spend time talking to his buddy about God. As we discussed the situation, it was revealed that this conversation occurred in a strip club, a place my friend had not visited since recommitting his life to Christ a year earlier. He initially justified his actions because his friend had been pulling away because they never did anything together anymore. After we talked, he began to understand that if his friend required him to engage in sinful influence to have a conversation about spiritual matters, his friend was not ready to have that conversation. He also saw that if he had so little faith to assume that God could not use other means to reach that person, he wasn't in the proper place to be an agent of God with that friend.

God will never ask us to compromise our holiness to bring someone else to salvation. We are to be in the world, but not of the world (1 John 2:15-17). Be wise in your faith and your zeal for doing God's work, but protect your relationship with God, and honor him in everything you do. Do nothing to risk your holiness, but do not cut yourself off from the people you can reach the most. Figure out a way to connect safely with sinners with whom you have the most in common. Love them, reach out to them, and share their struggles. Just don't share their lives of sin.

Prayer:

"Lord, help me to see others as you see them, and help me to see myself honestly. Remove judgmental attitudes based on other's actions and replace them with compassion. Protect me and guide me as I step out in faith to reach the people you have led my way. AMEN."

---

1 www.Quotationspage.com Results from "Cole's Quotables," June 2002.

2 The Quest for Character: Inspirational Thoughts for Becoming More Like Christ, Charles Swindoll

CHAPTER EIGHT

GRASPING GOD'S HEART

Luke 15:7
"I tell you that in the same way, there will be more joy in heaven over one sinner who repents than over ninety-nine righteous persons who do not need to repent."

Understanding God's character and his passion for rescuing the lost is critical to understanding our role in the salvation of others. He will go to great lengths to reach people, and sometimes the out-of-the-ordinary is exactly what is required to pull someone out of the ordinary. That is precisely why evangelism challenges the believer. You see, God never does anything halfway. His design is for the evangelist to be equally blessed in the process of another's salvation. If not, evangelism is simply a duty and not a passion. But, as with all Christian growth, the greatest blessing comes in times of faith when we have nothing else to rely on but God. That's when the greatest miracles of life occur.

After more than six years abroad, Susan Green, a missionary in Russia, has realized that God usually calls us out of our comfort zone in evangelism, and has seen how the believer is blessed in the process. She shares this true story of Margarita with the hope that through it you might grasp God's heart, and thus his passion:

Margarita's Story
"Kto eta? Skolka vremeni?!"
Startled by the voice, I paused in my rush from language class to notice a dark bent shape sitting on a raised iron sewer cover. Though it was summer, she wore a matted fur hat, a brown

overcoat, and wool leggings. These were tattered and gray, like the pigeons waddling around her feet and walking stick. The straps of a dirty canvas bag and gnarled fingers wove themselves around the stick handle at her lap. In clumsy accented Russian I gave my name and the time of day in answer to the questions she'd called out. Then, drawn as by an invisible cord, I sat down beside her and learned that her name was Margarita.

Despite the handicaps of her dancing dentures and my tripping tongue, our dialogue developed. Through the conversation, we eventually came to matters of meaning and belief, and she asserted that the sum and substance of life was *"zdarova"* and *"oospex"* (health and success). She did not ask for money, so I left her with a few words that sprang from an inner desire to somehow help her— *"God loves you."*

The following day she was there again. Now I wondered, *"Are those her only clothes? Does she have a home? food? a friend?"* and, *"Lord, what would you have me do here?"* Answers to the former questions came soon enough, but the latter would recur repeatedly for more than a year. At first I thought the thing to do was give her a Russian Bible. That's when I learned she was blind from cataracts. *"HOW then Lord!?"* I protested: *"I still can't speak Russian well enough to tell her about You. What do we have in common? I can barely understand her."* Yes, we seemed from different planets—or at least cultures, continents, and generations. She had to be over eighty years old! *"This wasn't in my plan, program, or our mission's focus."*

While I was struggling, unable to see the beauty in the blur, an answer found me. Someone passed on words of the prophet Isaiah that moved my heart: "Then the eyes of those who see will no longer be closed, and the ears of those who hear will listen. The mind of the rash will know and understand, and the stammering tongue will be fluent and clear." Perhaps she was to be a focus. Maybe we both needed to learn to see. I prayed for God to give me compassion and understanding.

We continued meeting on the sewer cover. I brought groceries and little care items, and Margarita reciprocated with such gifts as a bullion cube, a 1973 calendar, and even two gigantic brassieres. She worried saying, *"Will you have enough money left for your food?"*

Food? I found this curious until I learned her story. When I learned of her life, I began to understand her heart, and everything changed.

Born in 1914, a pure Jew, Margarita and her family of eight lived in Ukraine. After three perished in Stalin's deliberate famine of 1921, she and four siblings moved to Leningrad. Within two decades, WWII brought the 900-day siege of Leningrad and more starvation. (As a citizen of a country where hunger is associated with dieting it was hard for me to fathom!) Margarita's divorced husband was killed in the war. Her sixty years of work at a river shipping company had culminated in a recognition medal and a Russian pension of about $60 per month. Her existence had become isolated, except rare visits from a nephew, Victor, and me.

Every time we parted, Margarita insisted that I be on my way BEFORE she moved to go home *"where we'd have tea once her remodeling was done."* Hmm? Dropping temperatures gave me increasing concern about the existence of such a place for her. One day, I decided to linger quietly to look on from the nearby archway. Just then, two men wheeled up three huge bags of potatoes, and began to unload them near Margarita. *"Who's there? What are you doing?"* she called. They gave a brusk reply. *"Are there plenty of potatoes?"* she asked hopefully. They ignored her. She kept asking unaware that they had gone inside. The scene made me so sad I wanted to just shut off my hurting heart, which beat till it half choked me as I continued to stand in the archway.

Margarita moved to locate her cane, and standing up with obvious pain, slowly shuffled to the nearby building entrance. *"She must have a home in there!"* I rejoiced. But my heart sank by degrees, with each of Margarita's failed attempts to climb the first step. On the fourth try, she toppled backward, hitting the cement with a force that sent her hat flying. Her cane skidded away and she began to cry. I ran to gather her up. Disoriented, she couldn't understand who was at her side. Once inside the building, she resisted further help. I could only watch her agonizing ascent to the first landing where she hobbled to her door. As if things weren't bad enough, she dropped her key. I sneaked up and moved it into her groping hand.

Meanwhile, I too was groping my way in the dark; sensing how blind I was, how helpless, how desperate my need for the Lord to lead me. For example, the very next week Margarita was not outside so I decided to try visiting her flat. When the door opened, the smell and the sights of her unseen world overwhelmed me. True confession: I handed her a bunch of bananas, lied about needing to be somewhere, and left. She had shoved a little box of food tied with crusted lace into my hand. That night back in Pushkin, I removed the lid and a roach scampered out. Feeling "gutted," I sat right on my kitchen floor and prayed for her and myself. I saw better who I was.

Held up by people who prayed for me to be Christ's eyes, ears, hands, and hugs to Margarita, I went weekly in her "unremodeled" kitchen. I remember how she used to stick her hand right in the flame to check if it was lit for the teakettle. When she set down our grimy cups, roaches scurried across the table. Often I thought, *"Father, if it is possible, take these cups away from me."* Yet, it seemed His will for me to drink from the cup—keep going—somehow showing Jesus to her. I thought she would never see! Mostly she was uninterested or annoyed by the Gospel. Her spiritual eyes continued to see shadows and blurs, as blind as her physical eyes.

In August, Margarita's health began failing rapidly. She became suddenly bedridden and unable to eat. At different times my flatmates, Nancy and Pauline, joined me in visiting her. Once we asked Margarita if she would like us to read from the Bible. Unlike most times when I'd offered, this time she agreed. After Pauline finished a few passages, Margarita said, *"Another about Jesus."* The Word was read and Margarita repeated, *"Another about Jesus."* This carried on until in a satisfied voice Margarita said, *"It's true."* Those words fell on our ears like a kiss from above because with them we saw a change. As though light had burst in like a flood, her thin, yellow, hard face was changed.

Two days later her nephew Victor was there. Her condition was bad. She wanted me to know that she had something to say to God. She prayed, *"God I believe you died for me, and I love you with my heart. Have mercy and forgive me from every sin. I want to go live where the girls described to me."* I asked if she was in pain. *"Peace,"* was her answer. It was the last day she spoke.

The next four days, Victor, her 61-year-old nephew sat with her. On a Tuesday, Pauline and I walked into an awful presence of death. Margarita was still alive, but as if a corpse breathing. Both eyes were stuck wide open and unblinking. I was horrified until a thought struck me—behind those extinguished eyes was a soul who had sought God's salvation and seen!

For several hours we sat reading the Bible to her. Meanwhile, her breaths labored on so that we had an opportunity to share with Victor, and read from different Bible texts in answer to his questions. Finally, I whispered in Margarita's ear, *"Jesus loves you. He's calling to you. Go home."* We prayed for God to take her. Nothing happened, and with a pit in my stomach, we left. Only when I came home did I learn that after Victor had shown us to the door and returned to Margarita's room, she had died.

Eyes that had been closed are open even today. The blind received sight. I now see that the Good Shepherd never leaves his work unfinished. He supplies what is lacking and pities our falls. There is rest in his presence and fullness of joy.

Understanding God's Desire

None of us will ever fully fathom God, and I would not even venture to try in this book, but I must take a shot at the aspects of God's character that are revealed through evangelism. God is love—it is his love for all his creation that compels his desire for the lost and his mercy that makes restoration possible. It is his love and goodness that invites us to participate in evangelism for the benefits it brings to the believer. God is holy and just—worthy of our honor. As we draw closer to him through evangelism, we see that he alone is worthy of our worship.

The quest for understanding God's heart is your responsibility. There is nothing else more important in life than knowing God, which should naturally result in glorifying him. It was the purpose mankind was created for, but as Christians, we spend most of our lives and prayers focused on learning about God in context of his relationship with *us*. We earnestly seek God's heart to change *us*, but I believe we don't always begin our search in the right place. Our desire to please God is more often focused on our sin and how *we* can change to be more like Christ. We will always fall short of

141

our own expectations to be Christ-like if our growth in relationship with God is focused on ourselves.

If our heart's desire is to please God, we should focus on where God finds his greatest joy—and that is NOT the church. As difficult as it may be to accept, God loves you dearly, but you are not his greatest passion. In the parable of the lost lamb (Luke 15:3-7), Jesus teaches that heaven's greatest joy is in the safe return of the one lost lamb to the fold, NOT in the ninety-nine who don't need saving. We don't like to think of God's joy in these terms because our own selfishness desires us to be the only object of God's love. Since our salvation we are now one with Christ in heart and purpose. Therefore, one in passion—if we allow the connection by relinquishing our selfish desire to be the only child.

God's desire is for intimate relationship with humanity—we like to think of this as a great mystery, but God has chosen to reveal it to us. God didn't create man because he needs us. Being complete in the Trinity, he chose to create us anyway because love, the essence of God, glorifies and honors the giver. Our purpose is not found in merely "being," but being in loving relationship with our Creator. True life—spiritual, purposeful, and joyful—is found only in relationship with God and his family.

What's in It for Us?

Have you ever been around someone who is in the midst of one of life's joy-filled moments—getting engaged, having a baby, achieving a lifetime goal. Joy is infectious—you want to be with that person, hear the story again, participate in the moment because it makes you feel good too. Even if the person is a stranger to you, it feels good to see someone so happy. Now imagine that the individual is someone close to you—someone you love, someone you want to please. What does seeing and feeling that person's joy do for you?

What is God's greatest joy? God's greatest joy is being reconnected with sinners. It is the reason why God endured his greatest pain, Christ on the cross. His desire is never quenched. He seeks the repentance of sinners above all else. If God's greatest joy is when a lost soul finds him, don't you want to be there? Doesn't it make sense to be involved in God's greatest joy?

God's character—love, goodness, faithfulness—requires that all his actions toward us be for our benefit. There's always something in it for us. God does nothing halfway, so when we are in the service of God, we are blessed. Our participation in the process of bringing the unsaved to him is not for his benefit or for the benefit of the lost. We should evangelize for us! Sounds selfish only if you don't consider that God loves us and desires to bless us in everything we do.

God's Character

If you could wrap up the whole of what the Bible teaches about God's character in a word, that word would be love. Yes, God has many traits, but one trait transcends every aspect. David, in his song of praise (2 Sam. 22) speaks of God's character as "saving, worthy of praise, hearing, angry against enemies, rescuing, rewarding, seeing, faithful, showing (revealing) himself, shrewd, powerful, strong, perfect, pure, flawless, shielding, giving, gentle, preserving, living." True, God is a just judge and vengeful, as well as all the other traits the Bible mentions, but the underlying purpose behind all of God's actions is love.

God is just and unchanging because of love; he is shrewd and powerful and angry for our benefit. He protects us and never changes so that we can always know where he is and find him. Everything that God reveals himself to be is a byproduct of his love, so understanding his love should be the focus of understanding his character.

I believe 1 John 4:7-21 best outlines God's character, our relationship with him, and how we are to live our new life because of that relationship. If you remember nothing else of this book a year from now, I pray you remember this chapter. If you understand what we discuss here, not only will your relationship with God make more sense, but also your role in the lives of the lost will have newfound purpose.

1 John 4:7-21, NASB
7 Beloved, let us love one another, for love is from God; and everyone who loves is born of God and knows God.

We are called to love each other because God is the source of all love. As children of God, love becomes our nature.

8 The one who does not love does not know God, for God is love.

If we do not love, can we really be saved? God is not only the source of love (which he freely gives to all), he *is* love. All who love unconditionally and sacrificially (true love) know God because God is love. The essence of God's character is pure love. So we are both the object of his love and the demonstration of his love—that's why we were created.

9 By this the love of God was manifested in us, that God has sent His only begotten Son into the world so that we might live through Him. 10 In this is love, not that we loved God, but that He loved us and sent His Son to be the propitiation for our sins.

God made us able to love as he loves. We are unable to love "purely" without God because our heart had been hindered and limited by our sin. God sent Christ to replace our hearts with his. We are a "new creation in Christ" (Rom. 6:2, 4; 2 Cor. 5:17) as we live through him, realizing the true life for which we were created.

11 Beloved, if God so loved us, we also ought to love one another.

Now, because we have God's heart, we are to do the same for each other, so much as our position allows. We cannot provide salvation, since only Christ can fulfill that role, but we can have a considerable impact on the *process* of someone's salvation.

12a No one has seen God at any time;

Odd sentence to stick in here, don't you think? Seems out of place, but it is the critical element to grasp. God is always and everywhere present, and can be seen in all of creation, but many simply stop there or don't even bother to look. Most people are never quiet or alone enough in our culture to even take notice.

Because we are social beings, God can be most obvious in the context of relationship, thus in man.

> 12b if we love one another, God abides in us, and His love is perfected in us.

We are the manifestation of God's love on earth. God's love is made perfect in us when we become conduits of his love to others. His love is not perfected in us when we receive his love but only when we pass it on. The power of our own redemption reaches new heights as we become more like God through the unique act of loving others. We will never know God in all his wonder until we share his love with those who do not know him.

> 13 By this we know that we abide in Him and He in us, because He has given us of His Spirit.

Our expressions of God's love toward others confirm to us his presence in our lives. All doubt is removed as we experience oneness with our Creator through his Spirit.

> 14 We have seen and testify that the Father has sent the Son to be the Savior of the world.

Just as the early disciples, we can know the visible proof of Christ's successful role as Savior. We have seen it, we are living it ourselves, and we can testify to it.

> 15 Whoever confesses that Jesus is the Son of God, God abides in him, and he in God.

If you have expressed faith in Christ, you have this gift. Your salvation is assured, but better yet, you have the perfect love of God living in your changed heart.

> 16 We have come to know and have believed the love which God has for us. God is love, and the one who abides in love abides in God, and God abides in him.

What is your personal experience with God's love? Do you know and believe it in a way that you can share with others? Loving others with the love God has given us completes our relationship with him.

> [17] By this, love is perfected with us, so that we may have confidence in the day of judgment; because as He is, so also are we in this world

God's presence in this world is manifested in us because his Spirit dwells in every believer.

> [18] There is no fear in love; but perfect love casts out fear, because fear involves punishment, and the one who fears is not perfected in love.

If there is fear in our acts of evangelism, we are somehow limiting God's power in our life and trying to love under our own power, rather than letting God love others through us.

> [19] We love, because He first loved us.

We can only give what we have received. Unconditional, sacrificial, perfect love is only from God and only realized in communion with his Spirit.

> [20] If someone says, "I love God," and hates his brother, he is a liar; for the one who does not love his brother whom he has seen, cannot love God whom he has not seen. [21] And this commandment we have from Him, that the one who loves God should love his brother also.

Who is our brother? Is not all mankind? Could you possibly stand by and see a loved one destroy his or her life and do nothing? How then can we possibly be ambivalent about someone's salvation? How can you look the other way—be indifferent to another person's eternal destination? If you hate them you can, but then you can't love God, can you?

What is the ultimate act of love? Christ dying for our sins. It is unconditional (demanding nothing, but inviting everyone); sacrificial (complete giving with nothing received); and it is perfect (only God could do it because only God was pure of sin and motive).

If that was the ultimate act of love and we have received that gift, for what purpose? Our love relationship with God is only fully realized when we love others through their pursuit of salvation, God's greatest joy. If we never step into the process of someone else's salvation, we never fulfill the complete purpose for God giving us his heart. The act of loving others awakens God's Spirit in us and our purpose is realized. The gaps are filled; God smiles, and we are enveloped in his glory.

God Is Worthy of Our Faith

And without faith it is impossible to please Him, for he who comes to God must believe that He is a rewarder of those who seek Him. (Heb 11:6, NASB)

Evangelism always requires faith, and always grows our relationship with God. We must believe he desires more than anything for the lost to be found, and we must believe that he has changed us. We must understand that change in a way that we can express to others and then we must have faith that God can use us. We also must learn to discern his voice and go where he leads, even when it doesn't make sense.

Susan stepped out in faithful obedience to love Margarita—a woman she had nothing in common with. The story of Margarita accepting Christ was wonderful, but I'm also excited about what occurred in Susan. She experienced such amazing joy that she was compelled to tell thousands. Her relationship with God will never be the same. I know. I know because I've experienced that joy and walked away with an intimacy with God that I am certain could occur no other way.

God will go to great lengths to reach the lost, so he will go to equally great lengths to prepare us for the process of helping them. The beginning is in our blessedness. Our gift from God, his grace, is the change in our hearts that leads us to love God and love our neighbor. If you seek God's heart and pray for his desire to reach the unsaved, I promise He will always answer that prayer. As I mentioned before, allowing God to change us in this way is the ultimate act of worship.

Evangelism Is Worship

Worship, as defined by most Christians, is that time in the Sunday morning service when we stand up and sing. Those songs can be traditional hymns or modern songs, with anything from a room-filling pipe organ to an acoustic guitar or rock band accompaniment. We also would admit, when pressed, that one can worship anytime, anywhere, but rarely do we think of anything not involving music or singing as an act of worship.

There are enough authors, much more qualified than I am, to address the discussion of modern worship, but if there is a link between worship and evangelism, then this is the place to cover that connection. The Greek word for worship is "proskuneo," which means *giving reverence to someone and being obedient and submissive to that person.* Christ said that true worship will happen in spirit and in truth (John 4:23) and will place our wants, desires, and needs under the will of God.

In short, *worship is simply the act of honoring God.* It is doing anything that praises God and acknowledges his position and power. Therefore, there are as many ways to act out worship as there are moments in one's life.

Worship—honoring God

Acts of worship:

- Obedience and praise
- Action and thought
- Together and alone
- God-focused (or not at all)

Evangelism is the ultimate act of worship, the ultimate gift to the nonbeliever, and should be the ultimate joy for the Christian. Evangelism thought of this way becomes a far cry from simple biblical duty.

Worship of God most of the time refreshes the Christian spiritually and emotionally. Worship offered from an honest and humble heart enhances your relationship with God. Whether via connecting with God through his Spirit in communal worship at church and feeling his power in your life, or just living out a moment of obedience regardless of your emotions, you are moving closer to God.

Therefore, given these simple definitions of worship, it is fair to say that evangelism is absolutely a form of worship. If so, shouldn't the results be the same? If evangelism is actually worship, then the experiences should have some similarities. Shouldn't sharing your faith with the lost refresh you and draw you closer to God? Shouldn't evangelism draw you into a humble and faithful state, prepared to allow God to work his will in your life? As an act of worship, isn't evangelism something to be desired?

John Piper summed it up quite well when he quoted J. Campbell White as saying "Most men are not satisfied with the permanent output of their lives. Nothing can wholly satisfy the life of Christ within his followers except the adoption of Christ's purpose toward the world he came to redeem. Fame, pleasure and riches are but husks and ashes in contrast with the boundless and abiding joy of working with God for the fulfillment of his eternal plans. The men who are putting everything into Christ's undertaking are getting out of life its sweetest and most priceless rewards."[1]

Remember, effective evangelism requires compassion, consideration, and the Great Counselor. In other words, you must have the heart of God for the lost; be considerate of their personal spiritual journey; and allow the Holy Spirit to guide your conversation and prayers for the person God has directed your way.

Compassion is about aligning your heart with God's. Our Lord is sorrowful for the lost. He misses us. He desperately desires relationship with us. He has gone to the greatest of extremes to provide for our return into relationship, yet still most reject him. He has done so much to reach us, but still honors and values our freedom to choose. He honors mankind in every way, by respecting our choices, and wooing us to himself, clearing every obstacle along the way.

The rejected lover, standing with open, unconditional arms, waiting, day, after day, after day. He's calling out to his beloved, but he is ignored, sneered at, slandered, and spit upon. His love is so great that he never turns away, never closes his arms, and never gives up. His desire forever outweighs the rejection, and when one of his beloved falls into his arms, he rejoices in celebration more spectacular than anything imaginable on earth. He joyously welcomes her into his family, and he stands, once again, at the door and waits for the next.

Consideration is about listening and thinking. It is very active, but often silent. In Acts, chapters 17 and 18, we hear of Paul *reasoning* with the Jews. "As his custom was, Paul went into the synagogue, and on three Sabbath days he *reasoned* with them from the Scriptures" (Acts 17: 2, emphasis added).

This was a thoughtful interaction, not merely preaching. He spoke logically and persuasively, not as their superior, but as one of the common people. To get them to listen, he had to engage in conversation worthy of their time and effort. To reach some, he challenged their minds—for others, he went directly to their hearts. Paul was adept at discerning who needed what because he was following the lead of the Great Counselor.

When I speak of following the *Great Counselor*, I'm referring to prayerfully seeking guidance from the Holy Spirit before, during, and after conversations. Listening to God requires a response from you, always. That action may simply be waiting or remaining silent, but it still requires you to heed his direction. That is the great power and mystery of our involvement in evangelism— God's Spirit in us drawing and wooing the lost and enabling us to respond with his compassion and consideration.

God wants you to know joy and blessing in your walk with him. His Spirit *is* in you, tugging at your heart to look beyond the obvious into the hearts of the lost. He has miracles in store for you. He wants you to be a part of his greatest joy, again and again. Find pleasure in giving God joy, and your blessings will overflow. As you awaken God's heart for the lost in you, the priorities of living life take proper position. Loving with God's heart allows you to experience God's joy. Know God and know yourself.

---

1 J. Campbell White (1909), quoted in John Piper's *Desiring God,* page 188.

CHAPTER NINE

CHECK YOUR MOTIVES

Proverbs 21:2
All a man's ways seem right to him, but the Lord weighs the heart.

Why do you talk to people about Jesus? Why do you want to? You're reading this book for a reason, and barring settling a debt or dare, there is something compelling you to share your faith. What is your motive?

People aren't stupid. In fact, our media-manipulated, jaded culture is skeptical about everything. Most of us walk around thinking, "If you're being nice to me, I know you want something." The secret to relating to people who don't have an intimate relationship with God in a way that leads them closer to a personal relationship with him starts in your own heart. What is in your heart is reflected in your words, and the unbeliever's response will often mirror your intentions.

Test the theory. Do something openly nice for someone without them asking and see how they respond. Once a friend of mine washed the car windshield of a total stranger at a gas station in the snowy mountains of the west. I was busy pumping gas into my Jeep, and my friend decided to spend the time in a random act of kindness. The lady who owned the car walked out, caught my friend in the act, and appeared angry. Why would he wash her windshield? What did he want? She thought he was a total weirdo.

I've lived in numerous places, but being from Georgia, I'm still a "good southern boy" at heart. In major metropolitan cities such as New York, London, and Paris, I have received many a questioning scowl for helping someone with his bags or opening a door for a woman. This is no commentary on the merits of women's rights, or traditional southern ways, but experiences such as these have led me to a greater understanding of the cynicism of our culture.

People will not trust you if they don't know your intentions. Period. Does this spell doom for evangelism to strangers? Absolutely not! Intentions can be communicated in many ways. In fact, your intentions are revealed for you by your heart, and rarely require words. In fact, telling someone your intentions often creates doubt. It's like someone saying, "You should trust me. I won't lie to you." Yeah, right. The first thing I'm thinking is, "Why did you have to say that?"

Okay, so I'm a cynic. Maybe that's why I feel qualified to discuss this topic. We've all been manipulated at one time or another, so I guess I'm just like everybody else. Sometimes it's easier to hide behind our cynicism than risk exposure. The times though, when I have decided to trust someone and become vulnerable have been when I sensed genuine concern, sacrifice, or caring without expectation.

Because the woman at the gas station resisted the urge to drive away in fear and confronted my friend to find out what he wanted, she discovered he wasn't a freak and didn't desire anything from her. They exchanged personal information and later became friends. But she had to get a sense of his heart (his motive) before his actions could have a positive impact.

Evangelism is about your heart, and all your words and deeds will flow from that source.

Acts of Evangelism

Sharing your faith with a nonbeliever without the leading of the Holy Spirit can do great damage to the journey of the seeker and quench the Holy Spirit in the believer. When is the act of evangelism not only displeasing to God but contrary to his will? Can the act of evangelism become sinful? Let's investigate.

Story of Dawn

Hebrews 4:1-2

Therefore, since the promise of entering his rest still stands, let us be careful that none of you be found to have fallen short of it. For we also have had the gospel preached to us, just as they did; but the message they heard was of no value to them, because those who heard did not combine it with faith.

Staring deep into her eyes, I thought the moment was right. With a bold confidence I asked, "Do you want to pray right now, right here, to receive Christ?"

Looking down at the ground she sheepishly, almost inaudibly replied, "Okay."

"Great! Just repeat each line of this prayer after me. 'God, I know that you created me for a relationship with you.'"

Silence.

I looked up. "Dawn, are you okay?"

"Yeah, but I don't want to say it out loud. I'll just say it silently if that's alright."

"Um, okay. Let's start again."

I prayed and she listened. Did she say it? If so, did she mean it? Was she now saved?

We had been talking about Jesus after church on and off for months. For some reason she felt comfortable with me, and the trust that had developed between us allowed me to speak truth into her life and challenge her. She had struggled with witchcraft and had experienced several demonic oppressions. Her father, a friend of mine, was enthusiastic about our connection. After all, several people in church considered me a natural evangelist, so who better to befriend his daughter.

Her spiritual struggles were confusing to me, but instead of using that information to understand more about her heart, I tossed them aside and focused exclusively on the facts of Christ. I was a brand new Christian, but I was resolute in my desire to see her freed from oppression and discover the life in Christ that I had experienced. I was determined enough to do it at all costs. After all, her salvation was worth any sacrifice, wasn't it?

On this day, we sat behind the church for about an hour

discussing her objections. I found an answer for everything, and it appeared that she was out of hurdles. I had prayed all week for her salvation and was certain that I could get her to accept Christ this day if we just had enough time to talk. I pressed for the close.

Moments later, filled with emotion, I bid her farewell and we parted ways. I had hoped and expected to walk away as the obedient servant, triumphant in overcoming Satan's grasp on a lost soul. Not today. I felt more like the teenager that borrowed Dad's vintage Mustang without his knowledge and smacked it into a ditch. Why? I answered all of her objections; I got her to say the prayer, I think. I did my duty as instructed. You know how conviction gnaws at the corners of your consciousness? I tried to ignore the feeling and move on, but couldn't. God was trying to tell me something, and there would be no peace until I fully grasped this lesson.

There are three primary types of evangelism: dutiful, selfish, and godly. Which do you think I was engaged in when I talked with Dawn?

Dutiful evangelism is unfortunately the most common in westernized countries, and there are many reasons why this occurs. Coercion and guilt-motivation is a primary source of evangelistic activity and the reason why most efforts are proclamation-based rather than personal. "My pastor told us we weren't good Christians if we didn't share our faith." Well, there may be some truth to this, in a twisted sort of way, but the reality is that if you aren't a "good Christian," evangelism is not the answer.

Evangelism as an Act of Duty

Matthew 6

"Be careful not to do your 'acts of righteousness' before men, to be seen by them. If you do, you will have no reward from your Father in heaven." (v. 1)

"Do not store up for yourselves treasures on earth, where moth and rust destroy, and where thieves break in and steal. But store up for yourselves treasures in heaven, where moth and rust do not destroy, and where thieves do not break in and steal. For where your treasure is, there your heart will be also." (vv. 19-21)

So much of evangelism today is not so much from a passion for the lost as it is to fulfill our duty to the church. Pastors remind their congregations of their duty to fulfill the Great Commission. Christians know they are expected to share their faith—whether they want to or not! The truth in these statements is twisted and ignores the focus of this chapter—motive. Do we really think that a message dutifully delivered will cause heart change?

Most of us have, at one time or another, been the recipient of an apology dutifully delivered. You were wronged, the other person said "I'm sorry," but you knew that he or she was only doing what was expected. Saying the words doesn't make someone sorry. Genuine remorse starts in the heart, not with the mouth. Does an apology dutifully delivered but with no heart behind it draw you to that individual? Not likely! What you want and need to see is that the person cares about you before his or her words will change how you feel. Few will care what you know until they know that you care.

Duty is often done for selfish reasons, and the root is usually pride. It is selfish to seek the approval of other Christians in acts of service to God. It is as legalistic to evangelize for the purpose of recognition as it was for the Pharisees to announce their gifts to the needy, make obvious their fasting, and pray loudly in public.

Perhaps you are wondering if I am saying that evangelism is not a collective act of the Christian community where we team together, share victories, and encourage prayers—I am not! I'm simply warning you to be careful of your motives. Do you enjoy praise for a successful conversation? Do you want to rekindle that recognition? Are you comparing the number of conversations or salvation prayers you have to someone else? Be wary, because Satan can so easily twist something good into something evil. When you experience success in your evangelism efforts, remember that you are not responsible for that success. Even the saving of the lost can be used to create ugliness and sin if you are not careful.

C.S. Lewis in his fictional tale *The Screwtape Letters* demonstrates how easily a humble heart can be turned. In this collection of letters from Screwtape, a mature and experienced demon, to his young apprentice nephew demon, Wormwood, we see the essence of the dark conniving strategies of Satan. Wormwood is charged with derailing the life of a young Christian but has run across another in a series of challenges.

> My dear Wormwood,
>
> The most alarming thing in your last account of the patient is that he is making none of those confident resolutions which marked his original conversion. No more lavish promises of perpetual virtue, I gather; not even an endowment of "Grace" for life, but only a hope for the daily and hourly pittance to meet the daily and hourly temptation! This is very bad.
>
> I see only one thing to do at the moment. Your patient has become humble; have you drawn his attention to the fact? All virtues are less formidable to us once the man is aware that he has them, but this is specially true of humility. Catch him at the moment when he is really poor in spirit and smuggle into his mind the gratifying reflection, "By jove! I'm being humble," and almost immediately pride— pride at his own humility—will appear. If he awakens to the danger and tries to smother this new form of pride, make him proud of his attempt—and so on, through as many stages as you please.[1]

This scene plays over in my head whenever God uses me in someone's life and whenever anyone else finds out. The day you believe any person's salvation is dependent upon you, the sin of pride has taken hold. The moment you expect a pat on the back from a fellow Christian when sharing a success, you've allowed the Wormwoods of the underworld to manipulate a beautiful display of God's glory at work.

Manipulation and pride go hand in hand. Be wary, especially in your evangelism, when you begin to entertain manipulative thoughts about "closing the deal." Being true to the non-Christian you are sharing with means allowing him to decide, never coercing. Also, being true to God means never using evangelism, or the promises of God, for personal profit. Manipulation can be a product of ignorance, but is always an indication that your motives are askew.

Evangelism as a Selfish Act

Acts 8:9-24—*Simon the Sorcerer*

Now for some time a man named Simon had practiced sorcery in the city and amazed all the people of Samaria. He boasted that he was

156

someone great, and all the people, both high and low, gave him their attention and exclaimed, "This man is the divine power known as the Great Power." They followed him because he had amazed them for a long time with his magic. But when they believed Philip as he preached the good news of the kingdom of God and the name of Jesus Christ, they were baptized, both men and women. Simon himself believed and was baptized. And he followed Philip everywhere, astonished by the great signs and miracles he saw.

When the apostles in Jerusalem heard that Samaria had accepted the word of God, they sent Peter and John to them. When they arrived, they prayed for them that they might receive the Holy Spirit, because the Holy Spirit had not yet come upon any of them; they had simply been baptized into the name of the Lord Jesus. Then Peter and John placed their hands on them, and they received the Holy Spirit.

When Simon saw that the Spirit was given at the laying on of the apostles' hands, he offered them money and said, "Give me also this ability so that everyone on whom I lay my hands may receive the Holy Spirit."

Peter answered: "May your money perish with you, because you thought you could buy the gift of God with money! You have no part or share in this ministry, because your heart is not right before God. Repent of this wickedness and pray to the Lord. Perhaps he will forgive you for having such a thought in your heart. For I see that you are full of bitterness and captive to sin."

Then Simon answered, "Pray to the Lord for me so that nothing you have said may happen to me."

Simon the Sorcerer was much like me. After spending most of our lives working against God, we finally believed and accepted his Spirit. We both had zeal to learn and become a part of reaching others, astonished at the great signs and miracles of God. We saw the great evangelists and teachers and wanted to be just like them. We hung on their every word and followed them around like eager little school children.

It is rare that you would hear a Sunday message on these verses, but if you do, you probably will hear some disparaging comments about Simon's selfishness. Certainly, his offer to purchase the gift of the Holy Spirit was reprehensible, and the disciples' response was more than merited. Be careful, though, of judging Simon's intentions. He was wealthy and thought everything had a price. Yes, he was shallow, selfish, pompous, arrogant, prideful, and wrong. Simon was also one of us—a believer.

As a new convert Simon had experienced a radically changed life and was seeking to learn as much as he could. He turned from his career as a sorcerer, but something in him still desired those days of being in the spotlight. Seeing an opportunity to become powerful for the one true God, he leaped at the chance.

Why am I telling you this story? You say you have no ex-sorcerers in your congregation? When we first accept Christ, our hearts change, but the scars of our sinful history remain. Just like walking through a mud puddle, even if we get out of the mud, our clothes are still dirty. We first must identify the problem and then make the effort to get the remnants of sin washed clean. That may be as simple as prayer, or require prolonged counseling.

This seems obvious, I know, but the subtle impacts of sin from our past aren't quite as easy to see. They're more like mud on your brown pants. They may not look bad to you or anyone else, but they just don't feel right anymore. You may never even notice, but it doesn't mean they aren't dirty.

Simon may have had the best of intentions. The Holy Spirit was a good thing. Maybe he thought that he could finally do some good with his life. Maybe he thought he was called to be a disciple and wanted to get on with fulfilling his call. I can understand Simon's actions.

When I asked Dawn to pray the prayer of salvation, it appeared honorable to everyone I told. They saw me as an evangelist, just like they probably saw Simon. They probably paraded him on to the stage at meetings to tell his story just like I experienced. People were touched, and we both began to see ourselves as instruments of God, but something went wrong. Maybe more accurately, something had not yet gone right.

Both Simon and I, despite our salvation, were prideful people seeking accomplishment and recognition. Shrouded in the righteousness of "God's work" of evangelism, I pressed for the close with Dawn but the timetable had become my own. The need for closure was mine, not hers.

Over one year passed after that prayer with Dawn before God allowed me to pray with another person to receive Christ. For me, that was quite awhile. Fortunately, during that time, God led me to an understanding of why and to a greater appreciation of the joy of following God. I prayed with Dawn because of my needs, not hers. My selfish pride pushed to create that moment, not my obedience to Christ. I wasn't purely motivated by my desire, however genuine, for her to know true peace.

After that night with Dawn I had learned that it was actually possible to sin against God when sharing your faith. You can do everything "right." You can follow the commonly taught principles of evangelism, but if God hasn't prepared that person to receive the words you speak, if you don't sense that God is leading and you press forward anyway, you are going against God's will. You are actually disobedient in your attempt at obedience. I refer to this as an aspect of *evangelistic legalism*, and it is rampant among evangelical Christians. I repeat: *sharing your faith can be sinful.* Shocking, I know.

How do I know this to be true? Well, over one year later God gave me a second chance with Dawn and showed me what it's like when his Spirit is the one in charge. During that year I had moved from Atlanta, Georgia to Utah. Convinced that I would never see Dawn again, I pleaded with God for someone else to come into her life, as well as my own understanding and enlightenment. That year I found new depth of meaning in God's Word.

> Jesus gave them this answer: "I tell you the truth, the Son can do nothing by himself; he can do only what he sees his Father doing, because whatever the Father does the Son also does." (John 5:19)

I prayed for God's passion to become mine. I prayed for another chance, for a miracle of godly "coincidence" to bring Dawn and me together. I wanted to make it right. I wanted to see God at work and I truly desired Dawn to know the peace of salvation. It certainly wasn't necessary for God to involve me at all for Dawn's sake, but I prayed that he would choose to honor me with a second chance. Could I be so fortunate?

Longing for the companionship of my friends back home after

my first year away, I returned for a church-sponsored New Year's retreat in the mountains of north Georgia. Surprise, Dawn was there.

After talking to her and a few of my friends that knew her, it became obvious that the radical change I was confident Christ desired to provide for her life hadn't occurred. She was just as lost as before, but this time something was different in me. Was the Holy Spirit working in her heart this time? I wouldn't have to wait long to find out.

There were about thirty of us together on Sunday morning for a time of acoustic worship and prayer. While all eyes remained closed and all heads were bowed, I silently prayed for Dawn's desire to know Christ and thanked God for his power and faithfulness. I asked forgiveness for my pride and prayed, once again, that someone would reach her, resigned to the fact that it likely wouldn't be me, but hopeful nonetheless. Although the group prayer had just begun, I stopped and looked up at Dawn. Our eyes met and she motioned for me to move across the room.

When I arrived, she had already started up the stairs. Quietly, but confidently, she made her way with me in tow up one flight and down the hall where we sat facing each other on two small dorm-like beds. She purposefully gazed straight into my eyes and said, "Michael, I'm ready to accept Jesus Christ."

I was stunned and more than a little overwhelmed. Not willing to make the same mistake as the year earlier, I queried her, several times, in every conceivable way. "Do you know what this means? Are you sure you want to do this?" I summarized the Gospel and the four spiritual laws and asked again. Now she was being patient with me.

This time when we prayed, she asked in her own words for forgiveness of her sins and turned her life over to Jesus. It was complete. This time I felt the power of the Holy Spirit and was humbled to my core. Secretly desiring to run through the cabin screaming praises to God at the top of my lungs, I asked her if I could tell someone. She said "Not yet." Unbeknownst to me, God had answered my prayers by using someone else to help guide Dawn in her salvation process, and she desired to tell that person first.

Despite the burning desire to broadcast the news, I held my tongue but quickly found that I did not have to speak a word. The morning service had been over for some time and everyone was milling around, apparently unaware that either of us had left during prayer. I returned downstairs, allowing Dawn to collect herself, and soon found myself in a conversation with my friend Tim, far across the room from the stairwell. Abruptly, Tim interrupted and exclaimed with excitement, "Hey, check out Dawn!" I turned and saw Dawn starting down the stairs. "What are you talking about?" I asked Tim.

"Dawn just received Christ," was all he said.

Shocked, I asked, "How do you know that?"

He replied with complete confidence, "You can see it all over her face. Just look at her."

Because of my promise to Dawn I couldn't confirm what Tim already knew. But I clearly saw what he meant. She was beaming. Her face had a shine that shouted "This time it's real!" This time it wasn't about me. This time I allowed the Holy Spirit to lead the conversation. This time Dawn took the initiative. This time was God's time, and I was feeling humbled and blessed and free from pride. My role was merely to pray, be available, listen to God, and to answer her questions. Sounds easy, huh? In retrospect, I guess every fruitful conversation I have ever had with a non-Christian seemed easy when I allowed God to lead.

Evangelism as a Godly Act

1 Thessalonians 2:2-6

We had previously suffered and been insulted in Philippi, as you know, but with the help of our God we dared to tell you his gospel in spite of strong opposition. For the appeal we make does not spring from error or impure motives, nor are we trying to trick you. On the contrary, we speak as men approved by God to be entrusted with the gospel. We are not trying to please men but God, who tests our hearts. You know we never used flattery, nor did we put on a mask to cover up greed—God is our witness. We were not looking for praise from men, not from you or anyone else.

Paul and his gang of evangelists braved great opposition to reach those who were seeking truth. They did not attempt to please anyone except God in their service to the seekers. That meant they did not compromise their message to reach a broader audience, nor did they limit the confrontation. In addition, Paul undoubtedly had great opportunity to manipulate these situations for his own benefit if he had been greedy. But Paul went out of his way to remain focused, humble and effective. These men were confident in their actions because they knew God knows the heart of every man and they were committed to seeking God's favor and not the praise of men.

The fruit of the Spirit, which is the sign of a Christian in close relationship with God, is critical to your evangelism being fruitful. This fruit is evidence of the Spirit in us—and it is the witness of the Holy Spirit that calls and draws the nonbeliever. I know you've probably read this scripture a million times, but take a fresh look today. As you read through the list, check off those that were evident in your last encounter with a non-Christian.

Galatians 5:22-25
But the fruit of the Spirit is love, joy, peace, patience, kindness, goodness, faithfulness, gentleness and self-control. Against such things there is no law. Those who belong to Christ Jesus have crucified the sinful nature with its passions and desires. Since we live by the Spirit, let us keep in step with the Spirit.

Have you ever seen a cocktail tree? These trees are a combination of numerous citrus trees that have been grafted together into one tree. You can have lemons, limes, oranges, grapefruits, and so forth, all on one tree. It's quite a sight and very handy. A good cocktail tree has everything that you might need in citrus, but in the quantities that make it suitable for the individual. Each fruit retains all of its unique characteristics but shares the same trunk and root system, thereby receiving its nourishment from the same source.

Evangelism is just like that cocktail tree. The person God brings to you is drawn to that unexplainable light of joy and peace that shines from you. Your love for that person compels you to engage in a conversation and pray for the opportunity to share your grace story. Any response to your words or actions is in direct proportion to the kindness, goodness, and gentleness you display. With patience and self-control, the Holy Spirit guides you until the trust you have established with your faithfulness earns you the right to confront.

Pure Motives Bring Joy

Philippians 2:3-5

Do nothing from selfishness or empty conceit, but with humility of mind regard one another as more important than yourselves; do not merely look out for your own personal interests, but also for the interests of others. Have this attitude in yourselves which was also in Christ Jesus ... (NASB)

Even though I initially desired Dawn to know Christ for her own benefit, when I was focused on my own purposes, I was wrong. I was conceited and selfish and Dawn was still lost. God desired Dawn's salvation but equally desired me to be transformed by the experience. When I had finally relinquished my agenda, and my heart was so filled with compassion for another that I could no longer think about myself, he blessed me. When my needs became God's desire, my heart overflowed, and his Spirit was alive in our conversation.

Evangelism has very little, yet everything, to do with us. There is immeasurable joy, an intoxicating elixir of spiritual fulfillment that courses through your being when guiding another toward eternity. There's joy in obedience to the Spirit but not in the performance of duty. There is joy in actions that spring from a heart filled with God's passion for the lost, but pride and selfishness can steal it away. Joy that springs from the celebration of heaven over a found soul—that's the joy of evangelism. His Spirit rejoices, and our soul reverberates with the elation of heaven.

Be selfish in pursuit of the resonance of heaven's celebration. Bask in the glory of the smile of our Lord. Set aside your ambitions and pride, and open your arms in humility. Seek God's heart and there will be no room for empty conceit. Once you taste God's joy, nothing you can manufacture will ever satisfy. God's greatest joy is the salvation of his loved ones, and he's inviting you to share in their process. What a gift.

Prayer:

"Lord, change my heart. Give me your desire and compassion for intimate relationship with those that don't know you. Reveal any source of hesitation or wrong selfish purpose. Help me turn from that sin. Lord, I desire your greatest passion to become my greatest passion. AMEN."

---

1 C.S. Lewis, The Screwtape Letters, pp. 62-63, Collier Books, Macmillan Publishing Company, copyright 1982.

CHAPTER 10

GROUP PERMISSION— THE ROLE OF THE CHURCH

The concept of Permission Evangelism is being enthusiastically embraced by Christians across the country largely because of how it empowers the believer to share his own grace story and still honor the journey of today's unchurched seeker. This chapter addresses the role of ministries and the struggles they face in postmodern evangelism. Using illustrations from actual churches and ministries, I will suggest a few ways to successfully meet that challenge and demonstrate the impact a simple change of heart and some prayerful creativity can have on a community.

Mega-Church and Non-Christian Meet

It was like my first day at college. Years ago, my friend was scheduled to speak in a building somewhere nearby, but the campus-style environment of this mega-church required a day of orientation before I could find him. Already running late, I elected to ask the next stranger that crossed my path to help me locate the twenty-something service they called "New Times."

Along came a kind looking woman, Bible in hand, so I ventured, "Excuse me. Do you know where I can find the 'New Times' service?" Expecting a simple point of the hand or a "right up those steps" response, her reply took me completely by surprise.

"How old are you?"

"Excuse me?" I replied bewildered.

"How old are you?"

"Thirty-five, why?"

"Oh, well, you don't want to go to that service. You need to go to the thirty-five to forty-five group. Are you married?"

That was just too weird. Fighting back the desire to thrash her, I wrestled down my judgmental attitude enough to say "thank you" and excused myself, eventually stumbling upon the right building. During the service, my friend spoke on stepping outside of our comfort zone, trusting God, and connecting with our community in love—a great story of evangelism. I couldn't help but think of the poor seeker that finally gathered up enough guts, or found himself broken enough, to walk through the doors of a church and be greeted with an encounter like I had just experienced.

I desired to attend a specific meeting because I had a relationship with someone there, not because I met some committee-defined criteria. I also liked the style and music better at the younger service. As a seeker, I would have preferred that group regardless of my age. Unfortunately, I probably would not have been directed there. And if I had persisted after my encounter, I would have felt doubly uncomfortable—not only as a fish out of water in a church building, but also for breaking a rule by attending the meeting I liked. A not-very-encouraging start if I had been on an initial journey for truth.

Was the lady wrong? No, not really. She knew how things worked in her church and was just trying to be helpful. She logically assumed that I was a Christian because just about everybody there was. That's my point. Non-Christians, or to be more accurate, people that are not sympathetic and comfortable with Christian organizations, do not often venture onto the mega-church campus alone. Her assumption was correct, but the fact that it was is saddening. I'm not trying to indict the mega-church movement or endorse a particular method of worship. What I am doing is raising the question: "If a seeker stumbles into your church or ministry, what will he find?"

The Myth of Anonymity

I was that seeker at one time. When I initially began visiting a church, I would arrive late and leave early to avoid any personal contact. I eventually learned the perfect time to get up and go— when the pastor closed in prayer and everybody had their heads down. The program predictably had one more song, so I could beat a hasty retreat without getting stopped for conversation.

For several weeks I stuck with my avoidance routine. After a few times, I desired to get to know someone, anyone! But I couldn't step out on my own to do it. One Sunday I broke my routine and went to the bathroom on the way out. When I emerged, the service was ending and there was a guy in the lobby that approached me. He said he had seen me there several weeks but didn't know my name. He asked me what I did for work and eventually invited me to lunch with a bunch of his friends. That's when my journey for truth began in earnest and I started to make great progress. I may have initially wanted a measure of anonymity, and I certainly acted as if that is what I desired, but complete anonymity is not what I needed.

Although anonymity is a voiced desire of seekers, their true desire is relationship and community. If not, they would just sit at home and read about God, rather than visit a church to experience God. If the folks in your church are not too pushy and don't violate people's personal space, visitors will find a way to be anonymous if that is what they desire. But they also need to be approached occasionally. Some visitors may appear cold, but they really want to know they are noticed and someone cares. They probably don't feel comfortable hugging a stranger, and the glad-handing during the "stand up and greet your neighbor" portion of many churches may make them uncomfortable, but what will drive them away forever is, if after several weeks, the same people shake their hands, but don't remember their names.

I have a friend and his wife who attended a great church for six months and every week did the "meet and greet." They tried to establish relationships and even freely gave out their contact information. Nobody ever called. After six months at this 250-member church, they still had not even been invited to lunch, dinner, a game, or a Bible study. I'm not even sure if anyone even knew they were Christians. What if they weren't?

Another friend of mine travels a lot, and had been attending the same church for eight years. Every time she returned from a trip, she said it was as if she attended that church for the first time. Nobody knew her name and nobody knew she hadn't been attending for several weeks. She was certainly partly responsible for developing friendships, but after eight years, I have to wonder about the culture of the church that allows that much anonymity. How many active seekers have slipped through the cracks of these churches? How many are deciding this week to walk out of yours?

I always encourage people interested in evangelism to stand in the lobby about ten minutes before the service ends and look for the folks that consistently leave early. Come up with a way to engage in conversation. Introduce yourself. Start by just saying hello, then after a couple of weeks ask them to help you move a box or do something that will interrupt their escape routine and allow you to break the ice. The more they see your face, the more familiar you will become, and you can invite them to a casual lunch with friends or to an event outside of church.

I do not regularly consult on making a better church program. There are enough people with opinions and better qualifications than mine. But I do know the heart of the unbeliever. And understand intimately the mindset of the seeker. When non-Christians walk through the doors of your church, they are not only seeking spiritual answers, they are desiring something from community. You must still respect their journey, timing, and personal space, but the fact that they have ventured into the church or ministry setting gives you a certain level of permission. But there will remain a large majority of unbelievers that are not willing to look to organized religion for spiritual answers. With them you must be more cautious and more creative.

The Church-Alternative

As the number of seekers willing to walk through the doors of a church or ministry decreases, the need for alternative methods of reaching the lost becomes paramount. Salvation often must happen outside of the church for those without a positive (or at least neutral) history with organized religion.

Developing these new alternatives requires constant creativity to be effective. By that, I do not mean creativity in production should be the primary concern. Although it is important that your production not be cheesy, more creative emphasis should be given to approach—what works well to attract and appeal to the people in your particular location. Different areas within a single city require unique approaches and the process of finding what works is often a matter of trial and error. There is no such thing as "one size fits all" evangelism. And the needs of the new believer after conversion are just as unique and challenging.

Today's non-Christians are resistant, if not hostile, to anything that resembles organized religion and church, but we forget that their resistance doesn't disappear the moment they accept Christ. They are often still unlikely to attend church. Because of this, they are at huge risk of walking away from their faith unless they are immediately engaged in community. They need an incubation period where they can get their questions answered and engage with other Christians in a safe environment that is not overwhelming. The changes they feel from their conversion experience are sufficiently scary to make demands for immediate social conformance too much to handle.

Just as time and creativity are necessary to reach those seeking spirituality, but resistant to organized religion, it takes a different approach to help the new convert establish a healthy faith. I believe being in a close community of believers is a necessary step to a healthy, growing relationship with Christ, so the objective is always to encourage them into some type of regular corporate worship. Getting them to that point often takes time and a lot of creativity. Let's look at a three-step process that churches and ministries can apply.

Step One—Seeking Truth
Independent Event
An independent event is *nonchurch* in almost every sense of the word—no church name, no church building, no church songs, no church symbols, no church talk. This does not at all mean that you should eliminate spiritual discussion and overtones, but the key is to eliminate any sense of association with organized religion.

Eliminating the word "outreach" is a good start because it is rarely, if ever, used in any non-Christian context. The objective is to allow Christians and non-Christians to mingle, creating questions in the non–Christian's mind and conversation opportunities for the Christian.

Be careful to never "bait and switch" by luring unbelievers into an event and then hitting them with an unexpected sermon, however brief. Respect them—be completely straightforward and regularly tweak whatever doesn't work. With an event that occurs on a regular basis, the more diverse and eclectic the better. As soon as things become predictable and repetitive, folks stop coming.

Although the entertainment can't be predictable, these events need to be held on a regular schedule with a consistent location and time because most attendees will only come occasionally. Do not let this discourage you. It may take months and many scattered visits before someone feels safe enough to become a regular. It may take even longer before they'll connect enough to build relationships beyond basic conversation.

The primary objective is to build casual, safe relationships while encouraging people to explore their beliefs in a way that enables them to connect below the superficial. Make people think about aspects of life that the media and their other relationships do not challenge. Create spiritual perspectives to issues of life and encourage them to see the consequences of the decisions we make. Paint a big picture view of life so they won't stay caught up in the

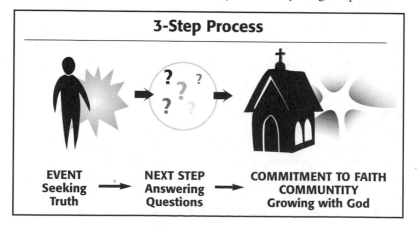

3-Step Process

EVENT	NEXT STEP	COMMITMENT TO FAITH
Seeking	Answering	COMMUNTITY
Truth	Questions	Growing with God

details. This will awaken inner desires to know greater truths and open the opportunity to lead them to where they can find the answers.

After a time, you can even invite the non-Christians to participate in the event. If you discover that a nonbeliever has a talent, encourage them to become part of the performance. Or, advertise a post-event open mic—you'll be amazed at what happens when you invite the non-Christians to be part of the entertainment. These types of events give you the freedom to involve nonbelievers in ways that are probably inappropriate in a church. Stretch the boundaries; break some rules; and allow God to move. Eventually, you can start asking non-believing attendees what they would suggest to make the night more meaningful or entertaining. You'll get frank answers that may help you reach a new level in your effort while showing the non-Christian that he is valuable.

Providing something of value to the attendees—entertainment or community at whatever level—gives them a reason to give you personal information. Collect addresses (e-mail preferred) or phone numbers to notify them of upcoming events. Start communicating and building relationships but be careful to never overstep their invitation. Always allow them to "opt-out" of the relationship and make it clear how to do that. At this stage, they must be certain you don't expect anything from them, but they must also know what they can expect from you.

Step Two—Answering Questions
Next Step
If you are effective at creating questions, you need to provide a focused opportunity for individuals to get answers. This usually works best as a personal invitation to a small group meeting or in individual conversations. In these sessions you can address questions about God, life, and spirituality from a biblical perspective. An informal gathering at someone's home near the site of the event works best—too much structure is often intimidating and requires a greater commitment than most are willing to make.

You might use a few components from the following to create your own invitation: "A lot of us get together on Sunday night at this guy's house nearby to discuss the types of questions we bring up here. We look at what God might have to say concerning these questions and talk about spiritual and philosophical perspectives. It's really laid back and we usually have one of the musicians from here play. It's mostly the same folks that attend the event, but it's smaller and more casual. You can just hang out and watch, or get involved in the discussion. We usually have some food there but sometimes we go out to eat afterward. I think you'd like it. Wanna go?"

As you put together what will happen during these group times, always give primary concern to the unbeliever. If you plan on reading from the Bible, make sure you have extra copies of the same version so you can give page numbers for guests who probably will not be familiar with how the Bible is arranged. Try doing some contemporary worship music here with a guitar player or DJ. Experiment with different ways to teach, get people involved in discussion, and pray. Feel free to let the guests direct the conversation sometimes, and answer questions directly.

Believers often resist this kind of interaction with nonbelievers because they fear being asked a question they can't answer. That is a needless concern—honest seekers will appreciate and identify with the fact that you don't know or pretend to know everything. When you don't know the answers, tell them you'll do research and have an answer for them next week, and then follow through. Some of the resources listed at the back of this book are good sources for finding answers to questions.

Make sure you remain consistent with start and stop times, but allow people to pop in and out when they want. Always do something casual afterward to ease any tension. You must make them feel comfortable by the time they go home, even if they aren't comfortable while they are there. The last emotional memory they have will be the lingering one. Make it a feeling of safety and acceptance, but remember that safety and personal challenge can coexist. Don't soft-pedal the message of God. They knew what they were getting into when they agreed to come. If they come back more than once, you know they are interested in truth, so don't hold back.

Salvation may often happen in this setting, or in subsequent conversations. As attendees begin to ask direct questions concerning

God, the Bible, Jesus, or how to live their lives, begin to meet one-on-one at a local coffee shop or cafe. Safe, public places are great to help focus the discussion without overwhelming someone. Now may be the time to introduce other resources for them to study on their own—you can always offer to get together to talk about what they discover. Seek to continually unravel the ties that bind their heart, creating obstacles to accepting Christ. Whether it is ignorance, a painful past, or expectations for the future, work to dispel their fears while continuing to provide small forks in the road leading to a decision.

Step Three—Healthy Relationship With God
Commitment to Faith Community
One woman I know told me that it took over twelve months after she accepted Christ before she felt comfortable going to church. She said her past baggage about organized religion and cynical skepticism got in the way of experiencing a Sunday service. She claims that after that initial year, she even started to look forward to attending church and now rarely misses a service.

Did her church change? No, but she did. Never underestimate the power of cynicism or childhood scars. Taking the step into a church building may require a gradual reconditioning over a period of time. This underlines the need for churches to create safe environments during the incubation period—the time between a person's acceptance of the value of the Bible and the need for salvation—and the point at which they can ease into church life. Sometimes this point is reached before the individual accepts Christ and sometimes it is not reached until after salvation. Because of the unique needs of today's seekers, churches need to provide safe entry points into the community of faith. Those entry points may very well be church-sponsored groups or events instead of church services or programs.

Example #1: Spy in the Land
Spy in the Land is an independent ministry focused on reaching a generation of spiritual seekers. It is based in Phoenix, Arizona, where it does the bulk of its work. But it also participate with other ministries elsewhere in the nation. In addition to providing

173

evangelism training and support for events conducted in partnership with churches, the leadership of Spy in the Land holds weekly events similar to those described in this chapter. Its leaders also speak and teach at numerous churches in the area.

The Verge is its version of **Step One**—a weekly event they hold at a local euro-style café and art gallery. Because their event guarantees attendance on the slowest night of the week and they encourage purchases, tipping, and advertise other events at the café, the management has given the ministry free use of the building for their event. As attendance has grown, the owners have discovered they are part of a win-win situation—Verge night has become one of their best and most consistent business nights of the week.

The event consists of a different musical guest(s) every week, usually only repeating every four to six weeks. Eclectic is the norm; in December, Christmas carols are performed by a Christian violinist accompanied by non-Christians on acoustic guitar and congas. They choose each week from a list of rappers, DJs, acoustic and electric musicians, poetry, rants, movie clips, homemade man-on-the-street videos, short stories, and crazy game shows, but always have a short, usually twenty-minute, philosophical, thought-provoking message. Musicians usually open the night and garner full attention of the audience and then perform another set or more of instrumental music after the message as background to a cacophony of discussion.

Two small teams of volunteers from numerous churches handle the production. Each group meets every other week to plan creative and production elements. They usually address a theme for three to five weeks as an enticement to draw you back the next week. Any given week, you may laugh, cry, get angry, or simply be entertained, but you will always be presented with a question of life.

Through months of trial and error and experimentation, Spy in the Land determined that The Verge appealed to disheartened and marginal Christians who would attend and more than likely invite their nonbelieving friends. In response to this discovery about their attendees, leaders began to add more Christian elements such as short biblical quotes that applied to the message. At the same time, presenting additional worldviews kept the edge to the event for nonbelievers. In short, the truth of life issues are addressed creatively, intellectually, and philosophically with the relevance of the Bible being introduced to individuals who may have never considered it a source of truth before.

Although Spy in the Land has never formally advertised this event, the regularly pack the house shows how the support of several local churches and word of mouth can grow a ministry. One church actually cancelled their own attempt at a coffee house event in lieu of The Verge because they discovered that mostly Christians were attending and not inviting non-Christian friends.

When word got out about a place that artists with original music could perform for Christians and non-Christians, and they had the freedom to do anything they felt led to do, the bookings abounded. In their first year of doing the event, they have never had a night without an artist, and variety is the order of the day. They have had professional, touring musicians with recording contracts, talented folk artists that have never performed live, and eclectic groups including an American Indian rapper on stage with a Mexican guitarist and a female diva that could be straight out of the '30s. You never know what you will see, but you do expect to be entertained and mentally challenged.

The Loft is **Step Two**. Appropriately named, it is held at the downtown loft home of one of the speakers from The Verge. Attendance is by personal invitation and is designed to create a safe but challenging atmosphere for discussion and getting to know each other at a deeper level. In contrast to The Verge, at The Loft the emphasis in the message and discussion is flipped, with the Bible presented as truth leading to a discussion of life application.

The gathering opens with acoustic worship, sometimes using handouts for group singing, but often just enjoying an individual performer to set a mood. Traditional elements such as communion may be introduced, but everything is well explained and put into proper context for the experienced Christian as well as the new believer and seeker. Teaching is done in more of a group discussion format using numerous questions. A typical study might look at the biblical account of the life of Christ chronologically so it unfolds like a novel.

Initial concerns about being too remedial or too in depth seem to have been unnecessary—even lifelong Christians seem to appreciate the community, diversity of thought, and solid application. They also enjoy the fresh and challenging interaction with less-experienced believers. Teaching duties are shared among several attendees, and even nonbelievers and brand new Christians are encouraged to teach or at least lead discussions.

The idea of untrained Christians or unbelievers sharing in the teaching may sound odd or inappropriate, but the intention is to take the focus off of the regular speakers and to create more of a community. I believe the Word of God comes alive when you teach because you are forced to see it from different angles, and with a sense of urgency you cannot create any other way. Most people will learn more by teaching than by listening. By putting everybody in the spotlight occasionally, everyone in the group is encouraged to get more involved. Because everyone in the group has shared the experience, they feel compassion for the individual leading on any given week. The community becomes a place of encouragement and healthy verbal interaction, thus building bonds of caring.

Occasionally, the leaders pick a topic for a short analysis and discussion to accompany the message the following week. Participants might be asked to do book and movie reviews that address a particular biblical perspective. Sometimes they are asked to read a particular passage from the Bible and search for other scriptures that address the same issue, or they may be given several scriptures and lead a discussion about what conclusions can be drawn in their own life about the character of God based on the passages. It's fun, challenging, and encourages community.

Step Three comes after conversion through The Loft ministry or through individual relationships with Christians in attendance. The Loft is not a church, and attendees are encouraged to attend somewhere else regularly. But by studying with Christians from numerous churches first, new converts feel more comfortable visiting churches, and the transition becomes easier. The leaders regularly meet with individuals for personal discipleship outside of the events, creating more trust, reliance, and closer community with every meeting.

In further support of the local church, new Christians and those reengaging with religion are encouraged to attend a new believer's class at a local church and pursue church teachings involving baptism. The Loft leadership has intentionally developed relationships with local churches in order to pave the way for new believers and have the information handy in order to help integrate believers into faith communities where they will feel safe. Whenever possible, they get to know the people teaching in a small group or class so that personal introductions can be made. They may even offer to attend the first group or class with them.

Example #2: *breathe*

breathe began in a very interesting way. Eight members of a Christian singles group at a large church in Greensboro, North Carolina realized they did not share God's passion for the lost. Convicted and desiring a heart change, they began to pray together for God's heart for the unsaved and for ways to reach them. After several months, the Holy Spirit had caused a significant change in their attitudes, and *breathe* was born as a Step One event.

breathe meets once a month at a coffee house near the campus of the University of North Carolina in Greensboro for an evening of music, totally wacky game shows, entertaining homemade videos, and one thought-provoking question, presented through a media element such as a video of man-on-the-street interviews. They do not have a speaker, but an M.C. directs the evening's festivities. This Step One event is used to invite people to other events—an appropriate activity hosted by their singles group at church or a different *breathe* event like an exotic meat festival. They give away T-shirts and generally have a lot of fun.

Although all of the *breathe* volunteers attend the same church, they are not formerly affiliated or funded by that church. The good news is that their church has not been threatened by their "out-of-church" ministry, but has actually encouraged them and allowed them to borrow equipment on occasion. *breathe* has its own website to help in promotion, but there is very little Christian or religious text available to the general public. To help with support from Christians, they have a special hidden page with a unique URL allowing you to view their evangelistic purpose, mission, and methods.

Their mission is to give Christians an opportunity to engage their non-Christian friends in meaningful conversation about life without pushing religion on them in a way that might alienate them. If the question of the evening sparks conversation that leads to a spiritual discussion, the non-Christian is invited to Step Two. Since the non-Christians have already met several Christians in the casual setting of Step One, Step Two doesn't appear quite so daunting.

The leadership of *breathe* (remember, they are young adult singles) purposefully takes the focus off of generating "numbers" of nonbelievers being impacted and more on impacting the personal lives of the Christians involved. Their secondary purpose, after creating an opportunity to build relationships with "pre-Christians" as they call them, is to *"remind ourselves and our Christian friends that lost people matter to God."*

As they describe their purpose, "The event itself, just its mere existence, reminds us and our Christian friends that lost people matter to God. Figuratively speaking, the *breathe* event is a poster, a poster that perpetually hangs in front of us, and the poster reads: 'Lost people matter to God.' Each month we—and many of our Christian friends—have this thought process happening: *Oh, that's right,* breathe *is happening next weekend. What am I doing to build friendships with pre-Christians? Who should I invite to* breathe? *I really need to step out in faith and invite Rick and Steve."*[1]

I love that attitude. The focus is continually on their own hearts and how they live their lives more than on the numbers they generate at an event. This makes me think that if the *breathe* event one day doesn't generate the numbers they think it should, they will be in prayer rather than simply redesigning the event.

Their **Step Two**, called **G.I.G.** is short for "Groups Investigating God" and is held whenever they gather a handful of people interested in getting spiritual or religious questions answered. G.I.G. is held in someone's home with guided but open discussion over snacks. They advertise G.I.G.s on the website but don't often promote them at the *breathe* event, instead inviting individual seekers who demonstrate interest.

Step Three happens through cultivated relationships and taking advantage of specific events that will appeal to an individual they have gotten to know. If the individual has a history with church, or appears open to the idea, he gets invited to church. If a person doesn't seem ready yet for church, he may be gradually introduced through a church-sponsored event.

Besides the fact that *breathe* was born entirely through ordinary Christians who dared to pray for a measure of God's passion for the lost, the most encouraging aspect of this ministry is the impact it has had on the church they attend. Historically a very mission-focused ministry, the church supports a great deal of international work and local community involvement, but evangelistic outreach events had rarely been successful in drawing non-Christians. From their experience, the *breathe* group determined that the distinguishing difference between the success of *breathe* and the failure of past efforts was that the Christians either lacked an active, open heart for lost people, and/or they didn't know how to reach out to the non-Christian.

In light of this realization, a new monthly event called **Plunge** was birthed. Plunge is designed to awaken a heart for evangelism within individuals in their own church. *breathe* leadership began with the singles group sharing their vision, communicating regular updates on exciting stories of changed lives, and even teaching methods for reaching the lost. The leader of the singles activities, not a member of the *breathe* team, told me that every member of the singles group, himself included, has been dramatically changed. As *breathe* shares their God-given passion, hearts are being changed and group activities have taken on new purpose. And the passion is contagious! I was recently invited to talk to a large group from the church about Permission Evangelism, further equipping this congregation to support and sustain a desire to reach the nonbelievers in their lives. Imagine how exciting it was for the *breathe* team to see a roomful of people eager to learn about ways to reach the lost and seeking to develop a heart that resembles God's heart.

The Need for Discipleship
Common among these ministries and any other Christian organization attempting to reach emerging generations is the increased demand for discipleship. The popular social environment with its gospel of complete inclusion has created an emerging generation

that lacks spiritual discernment. The ability to identify and choose truth amongst the myriad ideas that bombard us every day has been lost to the popular concept that all ideas contain truth. The ability to discern right and wrong has become blurred to the point that anything can be deemed right in the absence of absolute truth.

I have met many people in their teens and early twenties that have professed faith in Christ—have even attended discipleship classes, been baptized, regularly attend church, and even volunteer for ministry—but still entertain views contrary to Scripture. This is sometimes the result of not knowing what Scripture teaches, but also reflects a lack of spiritual maturity and resolve to counter the cultural influences of our time. Even after experiencing a life change through faith in Christ, they often try to strap on reincarnation, alternative paths to eternity, or whatever spiritual argument they read on the latest so-called Christian crackpot's website.

Here is a charge to the church! Immediate discipleship is critical for all new believers, but may need to be more prolonged with this generation to bear consistent fruit and keep them from chasing false teachers. They must not only unlearn a great deal, they must also learn to discern truth from fiction. We must teach them to think for themselves and not only question for *inclusion*, which they are pretty good at, but also question for *conclusion*. They must learn to eliminate options and focus on what will draw them closer to God rather than distract.

I have spent countless hours in discussion with marginal and new believers discussing unanswerable questions. They persist, but I press them to ask why they need to know. Are they choosing alternatives to faith in God? Are they refusing to relinquish their old life completely and embrace new life in Christ? I tell them that God wants us to be wise and to seek wisdom and experience, but to pursue wisdom for any purpose other than to grow closer to God is folly (Eccl. 2:12-16).

This is an issue that frankly caught me by surprise in our ministry. Even ten years ago the extent of the growth of the smorgasbord of so-called Christian belief was nowhere near as prevalent. An entire generation has been affected and if the cycle is not stopped, generation after generation will continue to seek "alternative truth" to combine with their Christian faith. There is no lack of false teachers, and we must help our new believers choose properly the teachings they should follow (Matt. 7:15-20). Very few church leaders seem to have recognized this phenomenon, so few churches are prepared for the mixed bag of beliefs that new believers may present. The natural response is to question the salvation of anyone that appends the Gospel post conversion. Those Christians who do that are missing the point. The problem is not solely with the person, but with our discipleship, or lack thereof. We must stay in closer relationship with emerging generations to continue the discussion post salvation. We must begin to reclaim the years that the culture has had more of an impact on our belief systems than God's Word spoken by God's people.

So, keep in mind, as you embrace and encourage a ministry to the lost, you must have a plan for discipleship as well. If your church already has a program of discipleship in place, check the curriculum and see if it is relevant to today's seekers of truth. Reevaluate the methods used to teach it and seriously consider conducting discipleship courses outside the church walls, in a home setting or at a café, to ease new believers into the church culture. If there isn't anything available or appropriate, check the resources in the back of this book or on the permission evangelism website (www.permissionevangelism.com). Remember, evangelism is not about closing a deal but encouraging a relationship with God. Don't just drop them off at the corner; make sure they get on the right bus. You don't have to commit to discipling every person you know that accepts Christ—that is why God gave individual gifts to believers—but you should at least make sure that they get connected to an individual or group that can grow them up in their faith.

Christian Entertainment or Non-Christian Outreach?

The greatest frustration I have found in coleading an evangelism ministry is not in the production issues, but in the recurring pattern of outreach becoming entertainment. This concern has been echoed in the many evangelism ministries I have consulted with over the years. I'm not talking about the message. I'm talking about events that were conceived to create dialogue with non-Christians but morph into something that is missing a key ingredient in evangelism outreach—the non-Christian.

Every ministry I know that does a regularly scheduled weekly or monthly event eventually gets in a rut that has nothing to do with the program or content; it has to do with the people. Successful outreach events, just like churches, are dependent on Christians inviting non-Christians. But too often when a bunch of Christians get together regularly, they tend to focus on their connection and forget the passion for reaching the unbeliever. It often happens in subtle ways and over a period of time. Remember, even with the incredible joys and blessings evangelism brings to the believer, it is risky and takes energy.

Watch for the signs. Are the same Christians sitting together every week? Are there only a few Christians making an active effort to engage in conversation with new people? Are there any non-Christians there at all? Are there only a few people that bring non-Christians? Is anyone other than the team involved in praying before, during, and after the event? These questions, especially the last one, are critical to identifying if anyone else has a heart for what you are doing, or if they are selfishly attending for their own pleasure.

If the answers reveal a consistent pattern and it isn't a positive one, do something radical—QUIT! I don't care if it is a weekly outreach that regularly draws a lot of people. I don't care if many people have been saved through your events. If your outreach has become Christian entertainment and non-Christians are no longer showing up, buy them all a VeggieTales video and send them home. Entertaining Christians is not your purpose!

Even as I write this, I am involved in a similar situation. A weekly event that I have been involved in has reached this point, and we just put the brakes on. Our attendance numbers had grown dramatically requiring a new facility to hold all the people. We were faced with the choice of taking it to the next level by searching for a new venue, continuing to jam everyone into the same room, or shutting it down.

Surprisingly, the decision was an easy one. You see, when we began, half of our attendees were nonbelievers, or marginal, uncommitted Christians. Many lives were changed, and a lot of people stepped into a deeper relationship with God. Then the patterns emerged—showing us that many of the attendees had not yet developed hearts for the lost. We had no choice but to address that issue before we went any further.

We could have continued to hold the events, trying to address the issue in other venues, but it wouldn't have had the impact we desired. Few would have grasped the magnitude of the problem and the importance of creating a change. We replaced that night with a study on God's heart for the lost and a great deal of prayer. I've done this before in a church and seen a dramatic impact. When only the leadership carries the burden for the lost, the best alternative is to direct your efforts to reclaiming God's passion.

I am confident that on the other side of this time of prayer and study we will emerge with a group of people committed to reaching the lost. They'll see evangelism as their best opportunity to experience God and grow that relationship. They will begin to understand how much God cares and aches for the children that deny their Father and miss out on his love. Lastly, when they grasp God's heart again, they will naturally take their eyes off their own issues and start to see what God sees.

They probably won't notice that last change has even occurred for a while. But as their prayers change and their requests become less self-focused, they will know love and become the very host of what they once sought. Then, and only then, will we invite them to reenter ministry events. I never know how long this will take with each group, but I do know that it is the one prayer that I can guarantee God will answer. If you genuinely desire God's heart for the lost, you will receive it. Once you allow God to place his desires in you, he has promised to give you the desires of your heart.

"Delight yourself in the Lord and he will give you the desires of your heart." (Ps.37:4)

Summary

These ministries operate completely outside of the physical boundaries of local churches, but provide outlets for Christian art and relationships with nonbelievers difficult to accomplish by any other means. They are not meant to counter church or contradict it in any way, but they do provide the non-Christian a counter-cultural perspective on Christians. These alternatives respect the journey of

183

those seeking spirituality but who reject organized religion. They ask permission, and they change lives. In the process, as examples of group permission evangelism, they are both challenging and changing the hearts of entire communities of believers.

I believe ministries like these support the church by radically challenging the commonly accepted social perception of Christians. The people in these ministries have learned that engaging the lost first requires engaging your own heart, and it is more about your heart than your production. Mistakes are acceptable because pushing the envelope is encouraged. They are fulfilling the Great Commission in a culturally relevant way, and they truly are wonderful examples of Christians who have become wise as serpents and harmless as doves (Matt. 10:16, KJV).

---

1 www.breathe-now.com/strategy/breathe.shtml.

CHAPTER 11

NO SILVER BULLET

Isaiah 55:9

As the heavens are higher than the earth, so are my ways higher than your ways and my thoughts than your thoughts.

A Word of Warning

This book contains recommended methods for initiating conversations with non-Christians. These have been tried and proven effective by attendees of my classes and myself, and I am confident will prove fruitful in your life. I am also confident that sometime in your life, one or more of these methods will not only be inappropriate, but possibly even sinful. Not inappropriate in a social sense, but very likely out of God's will for you.

We've addressed ways to discern the leading of the Holy Spirit in the life of a nonbeliever and how to listen to the whisper of God during those conversations. The latter is what I am referring to concerning the times when you must toss aside everything you have learned in this book about social appropriateness. What I teach are common ways to reach people in today's culture, being sensitive to where they happen to be in their spiritual journey. Sometimes, though, God is not socially acceptable.

God is all-powerful and can choose to manifest himself any way he wants. He can elect to slap somebody across the face with the revelation of his truth and use your hand, literally or figuratively, to do it. God may tell you to walk up to a total stranger and ask him a question about life after death. God may desire for you to get down on your knees and physically wash the feet of a person you've known but a few minutes. God can do anything he wants, and although I believe he inspired this book, it does not guide his actions, and he is not bound by anything it contains.

The only things that remain consistently true throughout every generation are God's character and desire for relationship with us. Every element of life will change save these two guiding principles that should foundationally order all of life for the believer. God is the ultimate opportunist. The difference is that opportunities don't just "present" themselves to God—he can also create them. He knows they will happen before they occur, and he works every one for the good of those who follow him. (Phil. 1:6) After all, if he can order the sun to stop in its tracks to suit his purposes (Josh. 10:12-14), he can certainly lead someone to salvation any way he chooses.

God's in Charge

Take, for example, the dramatic conversion of Saul. Nowhere in this book do I cover the miracle of God blinding Saul on the road to Damascus (Acts 9). That miracle is God-direct evangelism that only God can accomplish. That encounter is an example of the times when God chose to interact independently of a believer and then bring the saved into the company of believers. He did it then, and although it is not his primary modus operandi, he continues to do it today.

The point is that God can use any means, however socially radical, to reach people. What you learn in this book is what to do when God allows the natural order of things to take place through human relationships and man's nature acts itself out in the context of the leading of the Holy Spirit. It's about God blessing believers by including us in the evangelism process—not because he needs us, but because it draws us closer to him.

Please, never, ever ignore the voice of God because "Michael Simpson said in his book that it should be done such and such a way." Promise me that if you believe God is telling you to interact with a nonbeliever in a way that contradicts a method I've taught, ignore this book and do it. The test is a simple one.

When you hear that direction, answer these simple questions:
1. Is it in accordance with biblical truth?
2. Is it consistent with God's character?
3. Will it honor God and not you?

If you can answer yes to all three, act immediately. Do not delay in your obedience to the calling of the Lord. Let no man stand in the way of the will of God, especially you. Just as God can use all bad things for good, humans can twist the good things of God into something bad. The sin of fear grabs hold of anything available to excuse disobedience. The loser, unfortunately, will always be the Christian who misses out on experiencing the miraculous on the other side of the uncomfortable, where many of life's heart-changing miracles seem to occur.

Now, for the rest of your life, if God isn't choosing to blind someone in the middle of the road or use you as a battering ram for a nonbeliever's salvation, feel free to employ the teachings of this book. Always seek God's direction via prayer and reading your Bible. By studying God's character through his Word, you will grow accustomed to the sound of his voice. I pray that eventually you will be able to discern God's whisper from the sound of your old nature and it will become as clear as your own voice.

It might help if I gave you an example. In the late 1990s, when I was involved in strategy and marketing at a large software company, I met a woman named Tonya. We didn't really know each other beyond a few meetings and one short business trip a year earlier, but I recognized her in the hallway occasionally, and we would say "Hi." One day, though, I stepped out of the cordial and into her life because God suddenly called me to action.

I was sitting in a conference room meeting with approximately fifteen people, bored to tears. As I was staring into the hallway, I saw Tonya at the copier, and although my responsibility was to stay in the room for the meeting, I had this overwhelming urge to go talk to her. For some reason, God allowed me to see beyond her public smile into her heart. Through a conference room window I saw a pain that broke my heart. Her smile was false, and there she stood despondent and alone.

Unsure of what to do, I prayed silently. The simple urging to speak to her increased and focused. I was to invite her to church—something I never did without getting to know someone first. But I felt I knew all I needed to know. For some reason, my asking her to church was vitally important. I didn't have a plan, only a sense that I must act now or risk disobedience.

Surprisingly, the meeting abruptly ended and I stepped out into the hall just as she was finishing at the copier. I approached and casually asked how things were going, and she, of course, said fine. Then I asked if she had done anything fun over the weekend, and she responded no, and then asked me the same question. I mentioned something about hanging out with some friends from my church and commented about how much fun we had. I told her I was certain that she would like them and that my church was really different, suggesting she try it out. I gave her the URL and told her the location and time. Her face turned flush, and it appeared she almost choked. She said thanks, mumbled something incoherently, excused herself, and nervously scurried off. Well, that was not the response I was expecting. Nevertheless, I did not doubt my obedience to God's call.

She didn't show that Sunday or the next, and I did not see her nor hear from her for months. Slowly we began running into each other more regularly at work (an answer to prayer). From her response of subdued shock that day at the copier, I was certain God had struck a chord. Beginning that very night at a weekly prayer meeting, we all started praying for her desire to seek God. Every week I prayed she would seek truth and for God to provide more opportunities for us to interact, confident that the conversation at the copier was the beginning and not the end.

My church was a great distance from Tonya's home, so I hopefully began to investigate churches near her neighborhood just in case. After several weeks, I found a new church a couple of miles from her neighborhood and met with the pastor. I got to know a few people there and made sure I attended once a month to maintain those relationships. I wanted to be able to introduce Tonya to friendly faces if she ever agreed to attend with me. My decision to actively wait until her journey began in earnest proved fruitful in time.

Our first conversation about spiritual things ran dramatically counter to the effective methods I had developed and taught, but God had a different plan that day, and luckily, I listened. If I had reasoned with the prompting from God, I never would have acted. Although I initiated the conversation in an unusual way, our subsequent interactions still followed every principle outlined in this book. As a summary of the effectiveness of being able to communicate the impact of God in your life, and respecting the other person's journey, Tonya's story is as complete as they come.

Tonya's Story

My spiritual journey began as a random meeting with a coworker, Michael, at a copier in a hallway at work. I was acquainted with him but couldn't say I really knew him. He seemed like an intelligent person with a good sense of humor and a good work ethic—all traits that I respect. In the course of the conversation, Michael said he went to a pretty cool church that I should check out sometime, or at least visit the church's website. His comment seemed to come out of nowhere because we had never talked about anything related to church, and I had no idea how to respond. I can't remember what I finally said, and we ended the conversation.

As a child, my family attended church, but throughout my twenties, I did not actively participate in any religion. I felt I was a good and moral person and didn't need organized religion to "show me how to live," which is what I believed was the purpose of religion. Everything changed for me when my father passed away suddenly and unexpectedly, just a couple of months before my encounter with Michael. Losing my father was an incredible shock and shook me to my foundation. I began questioning everything I thought I knew about religion, mortality, and my purpose in life. I also realized that in spite of everything I had—good family, good job, financial security—I felt as though I lacked something more, although I couldn't define what "more" was. The result was a distinct sense of dissatisfaction and lack of contentment.

In an attempt to address this gap in my life, I decided to return to church for the first time as an adult. I thought going would answer my questions, or at least I'd confirm that I didn't need church. In addition to answers, I believe I was looking for some sort of comfort as well. I attended a local service a few times, but left feeling unfulfilled, so it was easy to give up on the whole idea. There just was no connection. Later I discovered that it was not the pastor, the worship, or the service that was at fault, but rather, my heart.

This all happened before the copier conversation. That exchange lasted only a couple of minutes, but it struck an emotional chord in me due to its timeliness and the fact that he had no idea what I was going through. I had never shared my thoughts about going to church with anyone; I hadn't even examined my own motives for wanting to at that point. Previously, I dismissed the idea of needing church as "going through an emotional time" and resisted anything I thought was too cliché, but this was different. I decided to check out the website, but my interest was superceded by my busy schedule, leading to the eventual loss of the information, and I did nothing more.

I continued with life as before but didn't forget the conversation. I ended up having more opportunities to interact with Michael, and we got to know each other better. We talked about all kinds of things, but interestingly he didn't mention his church or the chat by the copier again. I was aware by now that he was "religious"— my terminology—but he didn't raise the subject or put me on the spot by "preaching." That was fine by me because I believed that religion was very personal and individual, therefore I didn't talk about it.

Over the months, as Michael and I grew closer as friends, I became comfortable and more open around him. Then one evening in his office when we were talking, he told me a story about his past and made a comment along the lines of "I used to be like that, but I'm not that way anymore." I took the bait and asked what he was like now and why he had changed. Michael told me about becoming a Christian and how his life had dramatically changed since that point. I remember asking if he felt peace with his life, and he claimed to have gained an amazing peace and calm that he never had experienced before.

Then he shocked me by asking what I thought about God. No one had ever asked me that, nor had I asked myself that question, so I had no idea what to say. It became painfully obvious that I didn't really know what I thought other than believing that God existed. Listening to Michael was one thing; talking about my own feelings was completely different. That was new and uncomfortable territory for me. Luckily, he recognized my discomfort and chose not to press the issue.

Later on, I found myself (unwillingly) thinking about the question. I was unsettled that I couldn't answer it. What did I really believe and why? On a rational level, I thought Michael's story was interesting. It also connected with me on an emotional level, in a way that I didn't choose to admit. It was obvious that I lacked the peace he had, and was curious about how he achieved that. I was intrigued that he said he got there through religion, since that was a new viewpoint to me. I knew people who felt guilt due to religion, but not peace.

From then on, a dialogue began about God and religion. We met, usually over coffee, and talked about what a relationship with God meant. What were the benefits, what did God require of people, how did one develop a relationship with God? Initially, every talk was shrouded in friendly small talk, but eventually we always dispensed with the superficial pleasantries and got down to business. Throughout all of our conversations, I asked questions and Michael shared more of his own story—why he believed in God, why his belief was so important to him, and the ways it had changed him. I was attracted to the confidence and peace of mind he had and wanted that for myself.

A pattern emerged around our conversations. We'd discuss a topic until I'd get to a point where I'd get stuck. Either Michael would ask some question I couldn't answer, or he'd raise a concept that I couldn't swallow at the time. We always ended the conversation soon thereafter and would go our separate ways. The benefit of having our conversations over coffee was that I'd generally go home wired on caffeine, unable to sleep, with LOTS of time to think.

When I was alone I couldn't argue a point just for the sake of argument, so I had to get truthful with myself and examine what my hang-ups were. I'd have to decide to accept whatever was holding me back to learn more or reject it. Then we'd meet for coffee again, and I'd raise the topic of religion and pick up where the last conversation left off. Michael told me that God speaks to us in the quiet times, the gaps in life when we can hear his whisper. His whisper was sounding more like an air horn about then, and even though I was incredibly uncomfortable, I trudged on.

Through time, Michael began to encourage me to act on what I learned. He had an uncanny knack for challenging me when I was just being stubborn and there was no rational reason for me to NOT do something. He gave me books to read about grace, about the validity of the Bible, and about the proof that exists for Christ being God's son. He invited me to a church near my home. My initial response was to find some reason not to do whatever he was asking me to do, but inevitably, I would give in.

At the root of my resistance, I didn't want to believe he was right. I had lots of objections, but none that make sense to me now. Initially it seemed so "unenlightened" to believe there could be only one truth and one way to God. There seemed to be too much responsibility that accompanied a relationship with God. In addition to those objections, my biggest obstacle was my fear of change. Would I become a different person if I had a relationship with God? I liked myself and didn't want to become something new and possibly weird and close-minded. What would be required of me? Would I have to give up the things I had grown accustomed to? Most importantly, would I lose myself in this process?

Despite my fears, I continued to talk with him, read books, and even go to church, but didn't do more than that. I thought I couldn't make a commitment to accept Christ unless I was absolutely sure I could live that life. I wanted the contentment I saw in Michael for myself, but didn't want to change. I delayed because "I didn't know enough." Then one night, alone on a business trip, I awoke thinking about God and asked myself why I wasn't *doing* anything about what I had learned. When I was honest with myself, I realized I had just been making excuses. I thought about the reasons I had not accepted Christ and decided that the only thing that was holding me back was fear of the unknown and fear of losing control. The funny thing was that I knew no one is ever really in control of his or her own life when you think about it. My dad's abrupt death had taught me that.

That night I prayed to accept Jesus, over two years after the copier encounter. I knew what to say because we discussed those steps during our coffee chats many times. I knew it had to be genuine and from my heart. It was a spiritual, emotional, freeing, and even an intellectual moment that I will never forget.

Since then my life *has* changed, but not in a way that has made it any "less" than it was before, as I had feared. I discovered the peace I had been missing. I overcame the sense of missing an unknown piece of myself because I now know that piece was God. I am now relieved that I no longer *have* to control every aspect of my life. It is freeing to know that a much wiser being, who knows me better than I know myself, will direct my decisions so that I'll become the person I was created to be and have the impact I am meant to have. I am more confident for knowing that. I even look forward to going to church, which was previously a foreign concept to me. I still struggle with relinquishing control and giving into God's direction, but I'm getting better at it because I've seen how *right* (and there is no other word to describe it) it is when I do. When I surrender control, I feel calm instead of anxiety and confidence instead of doubt. To find happiness in being out of control says a lot for a control freak like me.

For the Both of Us

Everyone's story is incredibly personal, but Tonya's story is more typical than you might think. She attended church as a child, never made a personal connection, and lived with a negative perception of organized religion. She experienced a life-changing traumatic event that forced her to ask questions about her purpose and meaning in life and returned to church to seek answers. God drew her to his Spirit in a believer and spoke to her over a period of time, removing her fears and objections one by one. Tonya tells me she would not have prayed the prayer of salvation with another person nor walked forward at an alter call. She was stubborn and strong and needed to do it on her own terms. I think if God respects that, so should we.

Tonya not only accepted Christ. Because of the process she went through, she has quickly grown as a disciple. She learned to hear God's voice before accepting his gift, and her ability to discern his whispers has only increased.

For me, the experience was overwhelming, as it always is when I'm used by God to impact someone's life for eternity. I grew in my obedience to God, my ability to discern the movement of the Spirit, my compassion for the unsaved, and my humility. My relationship with God flourished and grew in direct proportion to Tonya's—all because I chose to be obedient to God. I abandoned the methods I have outlined for you in Permission Evangelism that day because God had another plan. I shudder to think what I would have missed had I not stepped out in obedience. I wonder what would have become of Tonya, and how much longer her pain would have persisted until someone else, more obedient than I, stepped up to the call.

I'm glad those questions remain unanswered. God's timing and Tonya's heart ruled the timetable, and I merely observed, remained available and vulnerable, answered questions, and prayed a lot (I was a sower). Because I understood the impact of God in my life in a way that I could easily communicate, I was able to give evidence of God's greatest miracle, my salvation.

People Like You Will Change the World

It is written: "I believed; therefore I have spoken." With that same spirit of faith we also believe and therefore speak ... (2 Cor. 4:13)

If non-Christians aren't walking through the doors of your church, don't blame your programs, your church leaders, or God. Building a Family Life Center, hiring a new speaker, and upgrading your Sunday presentation won't change your church's appeal to the lost significantly enough to pull them through the door. A friend of mine says "Evangelize or Cannibalize," and I tend to agree. Changes inside your churches, unless inside the hearts of your church members, will do nothing but lure Christians. They will not address the greater church issue. People like you, who are radically changed by the grace of God, are the hope for the church. If you don't feel comfortable inviting non-Christians to your church, and nobody there seems to understand the need, find a church or start a Bible study that will appeal to them.

Change your motives, and your churches will change. Change

your hearts and people will change. Focus on changing the lives of the lost, not your church. You can stay there, and be committed, but be more committed to reaching the unsaved. If anything gets in the way of you being a part of God's greatest passion, change your priorities.

If you are a pastor or church leader, I mean you too. Check yourself. How much time do you spend with non-Christians outside of your church? If not much, adjust your priorities. If your church does not have a heart for the lost, stop everything and focus there. Start with what God has done for them. Teach them to dig deep into the truths of God's love. Gather everyone together to pray for God's heart for the lost, and don't give up until dramatic change is evident and it takes on a life of its own. Give people the freedom to abandon ministry roles to spend time in the company of non-Christians. Allow alternative studies and events to occur if born of a loving desire, and don't try to redirect. Are you willing to abandon church programs for the sake of someone's salvation?

Make sure every small group or Bible study leader guides their groups in prayers for their families, neighbors, and coworkers who don't know God. Openly and humbly, share your prayers, desires, fears and successes. The enthusiasm of one with a heart of God is yeast that can permeate the entire group if encouraged. Hold each other accountable to prayer, risk, and stretch in faith. Make yourselves available and break out of the comfort of your "holy huddles." Stop looking inside unless it is at your own need for a new heart so that you can look outside and have your heart broken. Mourn the death caused by sin and cry for the salvation of others. Be changed by God. Love with God's love and *you* will become an evangelist. Attempt evangelism without a genuine love for the lost and you misrepresent both God and his message of reconciliation.

The Selfish Blessing of Evangelism
The more you spend time in the company of God through acts of personal evangelism, the more you understand God's heart for the lost and his deepest desires for you. To see God at work outside of you, through you, and in front of you, reveals more of the subtle prisms of his character and love than you will ever discover in personal study, prayer, or corporate worship. We know God best in the

midst of his greatest work, his greatest miracle. We know ourselves best in the presence of God—and that is never so evident as when we witness a seeker discovering new revelations or the transfiguration of the just-saved.

We are blessed beyond compare through our own acts of obedience in love and sacrifice for the lost, especially when we are called out of a comfortable place and into a place of complete dependence. We will never know God more than in those times. If you have never shared your life in the process of someone else's salvation, you don't know God as much as you think. You can't, because you haven't seen him at his best. And until you have seen God at his best, you can't experience your own best.

Throughout this book we have addressed the nature of people, motives, biblical perspectives, statistics, and methods; but all are for naught if done under your own power. I hope, above all, that you grasp this vitally important truth. You will fail without God. Your evangelism activities will die a withered death unless you remain connected to God's nourishing Spirit.

If you desire to bear fruit in your ministry activities and personal relationships, but are experiencing failure, check your motives. If you weep for the lost and your heart hurts to see someone in sin, instead of judging, hold firm and press on. Pray and share your struggles and prayers with others. Trust that God will reach that person. You don't know the end of his story, but you do know that God desires all to be saved, so you must act if given the opportunity.

If your heart is not broken in such a way, you have work to do with God. Praying for yourself is critical, and ask others to pray for you too. Don't wait for your heart to change before you serve non-Christians, just don't expect a lot of results until it does. Stop trying so hard. Listen. Ask questions. Get inside their hearts and see if yours changes. Learn about their life and struggles apart from any intention to evangelize and you just might be surprised. Put evangelism aside completely and just learn to love. God doesn't want your dutiful hit-and-run efforts. He wants you to bear fruit that will *last*. He wants you in relationship. He wants you to be in love: with him, yourself, and your neighbor. One Spirit, one heart, one purpose. Go, make disciples, for God's Spirit is with you always.

At the back of this book is a list of resources I think will be of great assistance to you. Of course, this is not an all-inclusive list, but I have personal experience with each of these sites and books. Also, check on my website periodically for updated recommendations (www.permissionevangelism.com).

APPENDIX A

Exceptions to the Patterns of Healing

There are two exceptions recorded where the individual did not have to ask for healing: (1) the healing of the servant of the high priest's ear in the Garden of Gethsemane when the religious leaders arrested Jesus, and (2) the raising from the dead of a widow's only son in the town of Nain.

(1) Luke 22:49-53
When Jesus' followers saw what was going to happen, they said, "Lord, should we strike with our swords?" And one of them struck the servant of the high priest, cutting off his right ear.
But Jesus answered, "No more of this!" And he touched the man's ear and healed him.
Then Jesus said to the high priests, the officers of the temple guard, and the elders, who had come for him, "Am I leading a rebellion, that you have come with swords and clubs? Every day I was with you in the temple courts, and you did not lay a hand on me.

This healing was to right a wrong and because Jesus wanted to ensure that everyone knew he was peaceful and did not resist. If Jesus was known to resist the capture leading to his eventual cruci-fixion, it could have been described as happenstance, or unfortu-nate. For it to matter in the way Christ intended, his death and the events leading up to it had to be purposeful, welcomed, and expected. Peter's brash act of brandishing his sword to prevent Jesus' incarceration, if endorsed by Christ, was completely counter to the reality of a man who willingly accepted that this moment would occur long before it was upon him. Jesus healed the servant to right a wrong, where an innocent man suffered, and to set the historical record straight.

(2) Luke 7:11-15
Soon afterward, Jesus went to a town called Nain, and his disci-ples and a large crowd went along with him. As he approached the town gate, a dead person was being carried out—he only son of his mother, and she was a widow. And a large crowd from the town was

with her. When the Lord saw her, his heart went out to her and he said, "Don't cry."

Then he went up and touched the coffin, and those carrying it stood still. He said, "Young man, I say to you, get up!" The dead man sat up and began to talk, and Jesus gave him back to his mother.

This second exception, surprisingly, is the only other time that Jesus sought out someone to heal and never required anything of that person to prove his or her faith. In this case, overcome with compassion and sorrow for the widow, he raised her only son from the dead. He asked nothing of the widow or the dead man.

Four other "exception" healings are also recorded—each contributing to a very specific purpose. With them, Christ purposefully set the stage for his eventual conviction and crucifixion. He didn't just go about living his life and "accidentally" happen to step on the toes of the religious leaders through unfortunate circumstances. The Pharisees and Sadducees were the only ones with enough power to convince the Romans in charge to convict him.

It was not by chance that the religious leaders took issue with Christ; he made sure it happened. In these four healings, Christ used the religious leaders, and their laws, to draw stark contrast to the freedom found in Christ, the new law. These four healings were used as teaching tools, openly confronting the laws of the religious leaders and challenging the Jews to forsake tradition in true pursuit of God.

(1) (John 9:1-3)
As he went along, he saw a man blind from birth. His disciples asked him, "Rabbi, who sinned, this man or his parents, that he was born blind?"

"Neither this man nor his parents sinned," said Jesus, "but this happened so that the work of God might be displayed in his life."

Later, the religious leaders questioned this blind man about his healing, and his story infuriated them. The religious leaders tried to trap Jesus but were only shamed by the declaration of a simple, formerly blind man unwilling to be manipulated. Truth dealt a heavy blow that day.

The next three miracles of this type were specifically mentioned as being done on the Sabbath. You will notice that the day of the week is not mentioned in regards to any other miracle of Christ. Evidently, the fact that these were on the Sabbath was an extremely big deal, or it would not have been called out.

(2) (Luke 13:10-14)
On a Sabbath Jesus was teaching in one of the synagogues, and a woman was there who had been crippled by a spirit for eighteen years. She was bent over and could not straighten up at all. When Jesus saw her, he called her forward and said to her, "Woman, you are set free from your infirmity." Then he put his hands on her, and immediately she straightened up and praised God.
Indignant because Jesus had healed on the Sabbath, the synagogue ruler said the people, "There are six days for work. So come and be healed on those days, not on the Sabbath."

(3) (Luke 14:1-4)
One Sabbath, when Jesus went to eat in the house of a prominent Pharisee, he was being carefully watched. There in front of him was a man suffering from dropsy. Jesus asked the Pharisees and experts in the law, "Is it lawful to heal on the Sabbath or not?" But they remained silent. So taking hold of the man, he healed him and sent him away.

(4) (Matt. 12:9-14)
Going on from that place, he went into their synagogue, and a man with a shriveled hand was there. Looking for a reason to accuse Jesus, they asked him, "Is it lawful to heal on the Sabbath?" He said to them, "If any of you has a sheep and it falls into a pit on the Sabbath, will you not take hold of it and lift it out? How much more valuable is a man than a sheep! Therefore it is lawful to do good on the Sabbath." Then he said to the man, "Stretch out your hand." So he stretched it out and it was completely restored, just as sound as the other. But the Pharisees went out and plotted how they might kill Jesus.

The Pharisees confronted Jesus about his failure to keep the Sabbath according to their rules. These healings gave Jesus the opportunity to confront the hypocrisy of the Pharisees and teach his followers the truth about the Sabbath. They also helped set the stage for his crucifixion by defying and angering the religious leaders. There was clear purpose in each of these healings initiated by Christ. But the majority of recorded healings by Jesus follow another pattern. Collectively looking at the rest reveals a possible guide for our evangelism efforts.

APPENDIX B

A Guide for Developing Your Own Permission Conversation-Openers:

1. List questions you are often asked about your life. (Example: What brought you to this city? How did you get into that line of work? Why do you participate in that sport?)
   a.
   b.
   c.
   d.

2. List any spiritual connections to those aspects of your life you listed in number one. As a believer, God is involved in every aspect of your life. If the spiritual connection isn't obvious, you may need to prayerfully explore it until you can make that connection. Completing statements like "I moved to be part of ..." " I play [name sport, hobby, or activity] because ..." "I went into [name profession] so that I could ..." may help you in the process. (Example: Instead of, "I went into teaching because I love kids," try "I went into teaching because I want to help kids understand their purpose and fulfill their potential.")
   a.
   b.
   c.
   d.

3. What are the milestones in your spiritual journey that connect to the life choices you've listed? These milestones *indicate a change* in your thinking, in your lifestyle, or in your values. (Example: I once

looked at work as merely a paycheck, but now I see work as a place to positively impact the lives of others.)

    a.

    b.

    c.

    d.

4. Keeping in mind both the spiritual connection and the milestones, list leading statements that answer the questions from number one but are open-ended—leading to the next question, and moving closer to a spiritual discussion. (Example: "I've read dozens of books about how to have more fulfilling relationships, but one book has helped me more than any other. I read it over and over again.")

    a.

    b.

    c.

    d.

5. Anticipate what the next question will be for each leading statement and write it here. (Example: "What book is that?" "What changed?" "What's different?" "Who were those people?")

    a.

    b.

    c.

    d.

6. What is your next statement?

    a.

    b.

    c.

    d.

7. When the Holy Spirit leads, what could you say that would invite someone to ask you to tell your story?

APPENDIX C

Outlining Your Story

Use this worksheet to help you think through the important points in your spiritual journey in preparation for mapping out your story.

Childhood

Sin by you or to you	Impact of sin	Emotions

Adult

Sin by you or to you	Impact of sin	Emotions

Conversion Process*

Contrary belief	Change in belief	People/events involved

Impact of God in my life

Change in choices	Change in emotions	Change in relationships

Describe your future with God:

Describe what your future would look like if you lived it without God:

*If adult convert, use initial conversion. If saved as a child, describe that process plus teen or adult reconnection with God.
1 http://sourcecounseling.com/List.html

APPENDIX D

Example: Childhood Convert's Personal Story

When I direct my workshops, the attendees are asked to tell their stories with no restrictions, and I take notes. The result is almost always the same unemotional list of dates and facts. When they are done, I do a "Q&A" to fill in the blanks and then read back the facts as they were communicated to see if I transcribed properly. Then I tell them their story as if I were he or she using the principles outlined in the book.

Usually I leave out a great deal of their past and make a few assumptions to pull in descriptive emotions. I focus less on the detailed facts of their life and more on the resulting emotional and spiritual impact of an outline of events. Of course, I usually must embellish the "impact of God on my life" section, which is where the "Q&A" comes into play.

The following story is taken from a workshop I taught, and is recorded as accurately as I can recall.

Jonathon's Story - My Notes (from original telling):

- Grew up in a good family (safe, secure, happy)
- Attended church as long as I could remember
- Strict and structured religious background
- Christian home
- Attended all vacation Bible schools, church camps, and such
- During sixth grade confirmation class I learned about Christ's sacrifice and baptism. We were invited to profess faith as a group, and I did.
- I "floated" for a while doing church stuff, but not much personal impact
- Working in ministry was helpful
- Two years ago, I attended a detailed Bible study
- Then a two-week mission to Mexico
- I changed churches for selfish and political reasons
- I've experienced contentment in my life, but it has been hard to communicate the impact of God on my life because it is all I've ever known as an adult

This was a difficult story to work with. Jonathon had been a Christian for over twenty years and had only shared his faith a couple of times without ever first being asked. He felt as though he couldn't relate to non-Christians and was a failure at evangelism. He was a lawyer and pretty reserved, so he was not very forthcoming with personal life experiences or emotions. After digging, I found that he had experienced a divorce a few years back that he completely left out of his story. He also had made two very risky decisions that both failed. These were the first times he had really failed in his life, and these experiences were devastating. After these experiences with failure he reached out for help from other Christians. Consequently, he had his first real personal experience with God.

There were many issues with making Jonathon's story impactful. He spoke almost entirely of his experiences with organized religion and never expressed an emotion or a reason to accept Christ. He also never communicated a real impact of Christ in his life or even the Christian community. Hearing this story would likely not lead anyone to seek a similar decision because there was no benefit expressed. There was little to allow them to connect with his life, although there were plenty of opportunities to make that connection. His story was one of self-selecting, rather than allowing the Holy Spirit to select for him. Knowing through the "Q&A" that he had issues with success and winning, and spent his life with other lawyers, I made some emotional assumptions and then retold his story quite differently. Note the change of emphasis.

How I Retold Jonathon's Story:

I grew up in a pretty religious family and went to church a lot. At a pretty young age, I knew God desired a relationship with me and even though I was a child, I realized that my life was lived selfishly. I prayed to accept Christ's death on the cross to reconnect me with God, but I don't think it really hit home until later in life. I had seen great examples of a life lived with God through my parents, but until I was tested, God never became personal. My religion was more theirs than mine.

I had become accustomed to succeeding at just about everything I attempted in life, and I attached my self worth to winning.

I made a couple of very bad decisions a few years ago, one of them a job change, and both failed miserably. For the first time in my life, I knew failure and real despair. I questioned everything about myself and my self-esteem was crushed. My marriage failed during this time and I felt all alone.

Throughout my life, I had looked to God only "as-needed" in times of minor desperation. Until that painful time, I don't think I ever really involved God in my daily life. I didn't know him personally and intimately, but now I understand he desires all of us to know him. It was through some new friends who were Christians that I finally understood God as Christ—personal, approachable, and forgiving. Their relationship with God was very different than mine, and I desired to live as they lived. I leaned on them and God for the first time in my life and was forever changed.

Now I see my life with God not as a religion, but an incredibly personal relationship. I have a friend and a father who desires peace and happiness for me. For the first time in my life, I have hope for my future that doesn't rest totally on my shoulders and accomplishments. My heart has been changed, and I know that I will become a more loving, caring, and understanding person. If I get married again I am confident that it would turn out differently this time.

As a lawyer, I live with the specter of success and failure every day, but I am learning to not base my self-worth on them. I know true love—and it is only possible through God. His love is completely forgiving, completely accepting, and incredibly challenging. It took me over thirty years to understand it, because I had preconceived notions about what it should look like. Now that I have set those aside, and seek truth in God, I am learning to see the world and myself through his eyes. It's an amazing experience that I know will never end.

That sounds like quite a different person, but after I told it, Jonathon agreed that everything was true. Will he ever be able to share that story with a nonbeliever? Perhaps some variation of his own making will work as well or better. I told him to pray over the following seven days for God to reveal to him what his life would now look like had God not been in his life. What decisions would he have made differently? I also told him to dig into his issues surrounding success and failure and where he found his self-worth.

What are the areas of his life that he has yet to trust God with? I implored him to dig deep into understanding the myriad of emotions that he dealt with concerning his divorce and job failure and what role God played in changing those emotions. Finally, I asked him to identify times that he knew God and recognized his miracles. He expressed that his daughter's birth was one of those times, and I was eager to hear about that experience.

Jonathon's story is a powerful one that could reach many people who struggle with their own self-esteem, success, failure, relationship problems, or belief that God is distant and impersonal. Just like Jonathon, you must trust that God will lead to you the people that will connect with your story. If they make it through the permission process, you can feel completely free to share a story this personal. Vulnerability, without details, invites them to engage and share their own doubts and fears. I pray one day you will experience the joy that comes with that kind of humility and sacrifice.

PERMISSION EVANGELISM

ADDITIONAL RESOURCES

For those who don't believe in the existence of God:
Mere Christianity, C.S. Lewis, Harper.
　Philosophical arguments for the very logical and very bright.
The God Who is There, Francis Schafer, Intervarsity Press.
　Scientific, logical arguments for the person who believes he is smarter than
　Christians.

For those who believe in God, but not Christ as Messiah:
More Than a Carpenter, Josh McDowell, Tyndale House Pub.
　Lots of facts and logic to address most arguments at a high level. Very easy to read.
The Case for Christ, Lee Strobel, Zondervan.
　Legal/historical arguments for the evidence of Christ. Easy to read, but long.

For those with "emotional" objections to faith in Christ:
The Case for Faith, Lee Strobel, Zondervan.

To help you answer tough questions:
A Ready Defense, Josh McDowell, Nelson Reference. (If you can only buy one book,
　this is it.)
Answers to Tough Questions, Josh McDowell and Don Stewart, Tyndale House Pub.
Reasonable Faith: Christian Truth and Apologetics, Dr. William Lane Craig, Crossway
　Books.

For New Believers:
What Every Christian Should Know About Growing, Leroy Eims, Victor Books.
Seven Wonders of the Spiritual World, Bill Hybels, Word Publishing.
Know Why You Believe, Paul Little, Victor Books.

Non/Anti-Christian Books That You Should Understand
**(The people you are talking to are reading them, so you should become
familiar with the basic premises and Christian contradictions.):**
The Celestine Prophecy, An Adventure, James Redfield, Warner Books.
Conversations with God: An Uncommon Dialogue, Neale Donald Walsche, Putnam
　Pub Group.
Living Buddha, Living Christ, Thich Nhat Hanh, Riverhead Books.